THE COMPLETE
MEAL PREP
COOKBOOK

500 Easy and Wholesome Meals to Cook, Prep, Grab, and Go

By

Debra Wetzel

permitted, or otherwise, qualified services. Seek for the services of a legal or professional, a practiced individual in the profession if advice is needed.

DISCLAIMER

The information contained in this book is geared for educational and entertainment purposes only. Strenuous efforts have been made towards providing accurate, up to date and reliable complete information. The information in this book is true and complete to the best of our knowledge. Neither the publisher nor the author takes any responsibility for any possible consequences of reading or enjoying the recipes in this book. The author and publisher disclaim any liability in connection with the use of information contained in this book. Under no circumstance will any legal responsibility or blame be apportioned against the author or publisher for any reparation, damages, or monetary loss due to the information herein, either directly or indirectly.

Table of Contents

INTRODUCTION

What Is Meal Preppi

Meal Prepping is the act of preparing meals to sustain you through the t... wait, I don't think that's right. Hold on... Okay, sorry, I got it now.

Meal Prepping is simply preparing some, or all of your meals ahead of time. It's like having those TV dinners that you would purchase from the store, except that you prepare them yourself, with better, healthier and unprocessed ingredients.

Not only does it save you time, but it also helps to ensure you eat healthier foods more often with the proper portions, instead of reaching for quick processed and pre-packaged snacks or meals that go over your caloric needs.

The idea is that when you have healthier things ready to eat, you will eat them instead of other potentially harmful foods. And it works incredibly well.

How to Get Started

It's important to remember to not get overwhelmed when you are a beginner. Too often people get bogged down in details when sticking to the basics will do more good.

Don't try to incorporate too many new things at once. For example, don't try meal prepping with all new healthy recipes. Start prepping with recipes you already know. When you feel comfortable, add more.

You see folks go on 'health-kicks' all the time, and what happens? They lose their gusto pretty quickly, because they add too many new things at once. They start a salad-only diet, going to the gym, running, yoga, etc — all in the first week. It doesn't work like that. You have to start small. Same goes for Meal Prepping.

1. Pick a Day

The first thing you should do is pick a day to prepare all your meals. For most, Sunday is the best day because it's a day when you are off work, kids are home from school, and you can enlist the help of the entire family if you need it.

More experienced meal preppers seem to like Sunday and Wednesday as their chosen days to cook and prepare meals for the week. Using these two days allows them to split up the week's prepping into two days.

In the beginning though, you don't want to prepare meals for the whole week. You want to start off with no more than three meals.

If you need a calendar to help you visually map out your meals use one. You can use a physical calendar or one on your phone. Just choose the one that works best for you.

2. Pick the Meals

You need to decide which meal you are going to prepare, whether it is Breakfast, Lunch or Dinner. If you are preparing for a family, then prepping your dinner meals seems to be where you would get the most from your efforts. However, if you are single, or cooking for one or two people, then you may want to try to prepare breakfast or lunch meals first. Ultimately, the choice is yours. You just want to think about it a little before you get started.

After that, you want to decide on the recipes you are going to prepare. You might not want to cook the same recipe for all three meals, although you can. But if you choose to prepare three dinner meals for your family, and they are all the same recipe, you might have a bit of a fight on your hands.

When choosing the recipes, think about how you want to balance the meals. For example, if you are trying to maintain specific macronutrient goals (proteins, fats, carbs) each day, that should factor into what recipes you choose. Knowing how each macronutrient converts into calories will also help provide more accurate information:

1g of Protein = 4 Calories

1g of Carbohydrates = 4 Calories

1g of Fat = 9 Calories

A kitchen scale can help with things like this.

They can also help you make sure you disperse each part of the meal evenly. And that brings me to my next point...

3. Use Proper Containers

You must use the proper containers. This can't be stressed enough. Good storage containers are really the foundation of a good meal prepping. How you choose to store your meals can make or break your meal prepping efforts. You don't want to simply throw everything into Tupperware bowls. That defeats the whole point of preparing things. Throw it all in one big box and what you'll have is a pile of good tasty meal.

"What Makes a Good Container?"

For starters, you want to be able to divide each part of your meal. You don't want foods cross contaminating each other. So what you need is a container that's air tight, with divided sections that are also air tight. This feature alone makes for better, fresher, crispier tasting meals.

BPA Free. This is a big one. You need containers that are BPA free, "BPA Free" simply means it's safe and microwaveable. You can check by looking at the bottom of your container and locating the triangle. If the triangle with has a number "7" in it, then do not use that container.

Other containers with the "number 7" may have BPA also, so be sure to double check. You should also make sure your containers are clear, and that they are the same size. Clear containers allow you to quickly see what's inside. Once you start preparing more and more meals, this simple feature will become invaluable. Same sized containers give you the luxury of being able to stack them easily and save room in your fridge or freezer. Put simply, you want containers that are:

- BPA Free
- Freezer Safe
- Dishwasher Safe
- Microwavable
- Stackable
- Reusable

IN THE KITCHEN

Start off, like I said, with just a few meals. Don't try to cook a whole week's worth of meals in one sitting. You may want to do this later, as you get more comfortable, but for now, just try to find your meal-prepping-groove.

Focus on simple meals. Chicken is a favourite among many meal preppers because it can be cooked in a seemingly endless number of ways. It's also easy to store and freeze. With just a bit of chicken and a few vegetables you can easily prepare three totally different meals.

Learn to Multitask:

Remember that you can cook lots of different things at the same. Use your oven space to its fullest potential. There's no need to place one thing in there at a time. Use multiple oven trays if it helps, or use aluminium foil to make dividers on one oven tray and multiply your efforts. Start with recipes that lend themselves to this type of cooking.

When planning your first shopping trip as a meal prepper, ask yourself if you have enough oven trays, aluminum foil and other utensils you might need.

Fruit:

Fruit is a great way to dive in to meal prepping. You can cut up different types of fruit and store them just like any meals you could prepare. You can easily make fruit salads or smoothies to go along with you prepped meals. Or you can simply start off with fruit preps only.

The Crockpot:

Okay, this one is obvious, yet so many new meal preppers overlook it. The Crockpot has been a favourite among moms for decades. Use it to make simple, great tasting meals then store them away.

How to Meal Prep

A Beginner's Guide

Meal prepping is the concept of preparing whole meals or dishes ahead of schedule. It's particularly popular amongst busy people because it can save a lot of time. Having pre-prepared meals on hand can also reduce portion size and help you reach your nutrition goals. This way, you'll avoid unhealthy options like TV dinners or takeout, especially when you're overwhelmed or exhausted.

And since it requires you to determine what to eat ahead of time, meal prepping can lead to more nutritious meal choices over the long term. Despite what people may think, there are various ways to meal prep, not all of which involve spending a whole afternoon cooking dishes for the week to come. You can choose methods that best work for you.

This article explores the most important principles of meal prepping and breaks down the process into a few simple steps.

Different Ways to Meal Prep

You may think that cooking meals for the week ahead will consume a big chunk of your weekend. However, because there are various ways to meal prep, you don't have to stand in the kitchen for an entire afternoon. Everyone can find a suitable meal preparation style.

The most popular ways to meal-prep include:

Make ahead meals:

Full meals cooked in advance which can be refrigerated and reheated at mealtimes. This is particularly handy for dinnertime meals.

Batch cooking:

Making large batches of a specific recipe, then splitting it into individual portions to be frozen and eaten over the next few months. These make for popular warm lunch or dinner options.

Individually portioned meals:

Preparing fresh meals and portioning them into individual grab-and-go portions to be refrigerated and eaten over the next few days. This is particularly handy for quick lunches.

Ready-to-cook ingredients:

Prepping the ingredients required for specific meals ahead of time as a way to cut down on cooking time in the kitchen. The method that will work best for you depends on your goals and daily routine.

For instance, make-ahead breakfasts might work best if you're looking to streamline your routine in the morning. On the other hand, keeping batch-cooked meals in your freezer is particularly handy for those who have limited time in the evenings.

The different meal-prepping methods can also be mixed and matched depending on your own circumstances. Start by choosing the most appealing method, then slowly experiment with the others to determine what suits you best.

Types of meal prep include:

Full make-ahead meals: You cook an entire meal and store it in your fridge or freezer.

Batch cooking or freezing:

Make multiple meals, then portion and store them. This approach is useful for recipes you can easily cook in large amounts (like big pots of soup, rice, or mashed sweet potatoes).

Meals for one:

Prepare food and portion it in single-serving containers. Usually enough to last a few days.

Ingredient prep:

For people who like to cook and serve food all at once, just prep parts of recipes. Chop veggies, mix spices, or marinade meat in advance to save time when you're ready to cook.

Why Should You Meal Prep?

Learning how to meal prep will save you time, but it also saves money and reduces waste. And unlike processed meals, this method gives you total control over what goes in your food — perfect for anyone who wants to stay on track with their health goals.

Is meal prep for everyone?

Meal prep can benefit people watching their macros or trying to cut down their cook time during the week.

However, some forms of meal prep may not be for everyone. When you cook and store your meals, they may ferment just long enough to cause a negative reaction. How? When packed and stored, leftover food can release histamines as a by-product of the fermentation process. If you're particularly sensitive to these compounds, your leftovers could cause brain fog and fatigue.

How Long Are Leftovers Good for?

What You Should Know Before You Meal Prep

Since everyone's histamine tolerance is different, it's still worth it to try meal prep, avoid high-histamine foods when you cook, and see if the process works for you. Consider meal prepping for a shorter time frame, or prepping single ingredients instead of full meals.

What foods can I meal prep?

You can meal prep any food that holds up well in storage and tastes palatable to you after a few days in the refrigerator. Cooked meat, roasted vegetables, soups, sauces, nuts, and stiff raw vegetables make good bases for meal prep recipes. But you can't meal prep everything. Soft vegetables, cut fruit, and crunchy food like crackers will only get softer in your refrigerator — making them less ideal choices for meal prep.

If you're new to meal prep, think about how you'll reheat food. Will you only have access to a microwave at mealtime, or can you use a stovetop or oven? Consider recipes that you can enjoy cold or gently reheat so you don't risk damaging fats and proteins in your food. Most importantly, choose recipes that you already enjoy leftover and can cook with ease. Then you can branch out with new recipes and food pairings. Keep it simple to start so you don't find yourself wasting food.

HOW TO MEAL PREP

First step:

Use quality food storage containers to keep meal prep food hot or cold. Thermal, stainless steel containers are the ideal solution for keeping food warm or chilled, and come in a variety of sizes. You can refrigerate them ahead of time or warm them with boiling water before adding cold or hot foods to make them last even longer. Glassware is the safest solution of all, as long as you plan on enjoying your meal cold and can handle it carefully.

Reusable plastics and plastic bags are never recommended for packing meal prep foods. Aside from carcinogenic BPA, even non-BPA plastics can contain estrogenic chemicals that leach into your food and mess with your hormones. And if you heat these plastics in the microwave, you're also adding radiation to the mix. Avoid storing food in plastic whenever you can to keep your meal prep dishes optimal.

Choose recipes and build your menu. With simple recipes in hand, decide what you'll cook for the week and schedule the days of the week when you want to enjoy your meals. Take stock of what you need for those recipes, plus any missing essentials you need like spices or ghee, and make your grocery list.

Schedule time for meal prep. You can't meal prep without prep time. Schedule a window one to two days per week to prep your meals. If you multitask a little (use your oven and stove top to prep more than one food at once, for example), you'll cut down on time even more.

What Really Causes Heartburn

- Fibre for Fat Burning and a Stronger Gut
- Dirty Keto: Why Dairy Isn't as Keto Friendly as You Think
- 12 Best Paleo Foods You Can Find

Food safety

There are no hard and fast rules for how long your food will stay fresh. The safety of your meal prep depends a lot on your refrigerator, how you packed it, and the quality of your ingredients.

Start with the FDA's guidelines for fridge and freezer storage to inform how long you can store meal prep foods, and practice common sense when you pack food so it can last longer. Use divided containers to avoid cross-contamination or flavour contamination, and pack wet food separate from dry food. Use ice packs to keep cold dishes cold, and pre-warmed insulated containers to keep hot foods hot. And of course, clean your hands and produce before you cook.

Most meal prep meals will last between 3 to 5 days in the fridge. If you want to meal prep for the whole week, you'll want to schedule two days a week to do so such as Sunday and Wednesday to keep food as fresh as possible.

(Should I meal prep if I don't like eating the same thing every day?)

Prepping the exact same meal every day can save a lot of time, but it also gets boring. If you tired of eating the same meals over and over, make small tweaks to your meal prep to make each dish a little different. For example, swap in different veggies, sauces, or garnishes for each container to keep things interesting.

Alternatively, you can prep and freeze multiple recipes ahead of time. Then, thaw one or two containers in the refrigerator every day so you can enjoy different dishes throughout the week.

Avoiding common mistakes?

Keep meal prep simple. For beginners, start simple. Make one-pot recipes or focus on one main dish, and avoid the temptation to spend a whole day cooking elaborate meals. Too many recipes can complicate your meal prep fast, and you may not want to do it again if it was too hard the first time. Try making just one recipe ahead of time, then meal prep additional dishes when you get comfortable.

Prep balanced meals. Depending on your diet and health goals, plan meals that will keep you satisfied. It's easy to make a big bowl of chili for lunch, but it wouldn't serve as a complete meal for most people. Make sure you get enough of the right food groups to fill out your macros.

Cook recipes you'll actually eat. As long as your meal prep dishes are balanced, you don't need to branch out of your comfort zone. For beginners, make recipes you know you'll love — anything less could result in wasted food (and wasted time).

Make enough food. Make sure you prep enough food to fit your plan. Furthermore, keep your schedule in mind — events from work lunches to happy hours can interfere with mealtime, so anticipate whether you truly need to meal prep every day.

Meal Prep Must Haves

1. A Sharpie is a necessity for labelling the meals you prep so you know what is in the freezer.

2. Make sure you have gallon size freezer bags on hand for storing your meals.

3. A roll of foil is great for covering throw away casserole dishes tightly.

4. Some recipes may need parchment paper to prevent sticking when cooking.

5. Freezer bag holders work for assembly but also soups, sauces, and other chopped favourites.

6. We love this collapsible colander that works wonders for rinsing veggies and fruits prior to assembly.

7. If you run short on time you can defrost just about anything in a jiffy with a thaw board.

8. These freezer casserole dishes are just right for casseroles and such and they work well in the freezer with no worry for shattering.

9. Meal Prep Containers are great if you assembling smaller portions for smaller families or just a quick easy meal.

10. Glad Ovenware is a disposable option for freezer meal assembly.

11. When prepping you have to have measuring cups and measuring spoons help for adding all the right ingredients.

12. A slow cooker is a saving grace for whipping up those meals you have assembled.

13. My instant pot is the quickest and easiest way to cook in no time.

14. Having a good-sized stock pot on hand makes for boiling things up pretty easy.

15. We love these baking sheets for those delicious sheet pan dinners!

16. Keep mixing bowls counter top for mixing marinades and veggies.

17. We love these cutting boards for assembling because they have handy labels for what they are used for.

18. A set of sharp knives makes for chopping super simple.

19. If you are storing away seasoned meat or other items use a Food saver to make things freezer friendly.

20. Having a kitchen timer on hand is wonderful for keeping track of multiple tasks while you are prepping.

21. We like to precook ground beef and other things in a sauté pan prior to assembly.

22. You can shred, chop, and puree just about anything when using a food processor like this one.

23. If you are measuring out foods for health reasons or precision a kitchen scale is perfect!

BREAKFAST RECIPES

Egg and Sausage McMuffin

Preparation time: 20 minutes

Cooking time20 minutes

Gross time: 40 minutes

Serves: 4 to 6 people

Recipe Ingredients:

- 1 tablespoon of olive oil, divided
- 1 pound of ground chicken or turkey
- 1 tablespoon of fennel seeds
- 1 teaspoon of paprika
- 1 teaspoon of garlic powder
- 1 teaspoon of salt
- ½ teaspoon of pepper
- 6 eggs
- 6 cheddar cheese slices
- 6 English muffins

Cooking Instructions:

1. In a large bowl mix together ground turkey, fennel, paprika, garlic powder, salt and pepper.

2. Form 6 patties. Preheat 1 tablespoon of olive oil over med-high heat and then add patties to skillet.

3. Cook for about 5 minutes per side until sausage patties are cooked all the way through.

4. Meanwhile, lightly toast English muffins in a toaster, then add cheese slices to bottom of muffins.

5. Remove sausages from heat and add them on top of cheese slices on muffins. Wipe frying pan clean with a paper towel, spray with cooking spray.

6. Turn heat to med-low. Crack eggs into egg rings, ensuring that the rings are firmly touching bottom of skillet so eggs maintain a round shape, and break yolk.

7. Cover skillet with lid and cook eggs for about 4 to 5 minutes or until eggs are firm, then add on top of sausages and top with remaining English muffin buns.

8. Serve and enjoy!

Quinoa Breakfast

Preparation time: 5 minutes

Cooking time: 15 minutes

Overall time: 20 minutes

Serves: 2 to 4 people

Recipe Ingredients:

- 1 cup of quinoa
- 2 cups of almond milk * see notes
- ½ tsp. of ground cinnamon
- ¼ tsp. of ground cardamom
- 2 tbsp. of maple syrup
- 4 cups of mixed berries
- 4 tbsp. of sliced almonds

Cooking Instructions:

1. In a medium pot, combine the quinoa, almond milk, cinnamon, and cardamom.

2. Bring to a boil, reduce heat and simmer for about 15 or so minutes, until the quinoa is cooked through allow quinoa to Cool.

3. Stir in the maple syrup, and divide into four containers: ¾ cup of cooked quinoa, 1 cup of fruit, 1 tablespoon sliced almonds.

4. Serve immediately and Enjoy!

Oven-Baked Starbucks Egg Bites

Preparation time: 15 minutes

Cooking time: 1 hour

Gross time: 1 hour 15 minutes

Serves: 5 to 7 people

Recipe Ingredients:

- 1 tablespoon of olive oil (to grease egg tray)
- 16 eggs, whisked
- 1 cup of bacon or turkey bacon, cooked and chopped
- 1 cup of gruyere cheese or aged cheddar, shredded
- Egg White and Red Pepper
- 1 tablespoon of olive oil (to grease egg tray)
- 4 cups of egg whites
- 1 cup of roasted red peppers, diced
- 1 cup of spinach, finely chopped
- 1 cup of Monterey jack cheese, shredded

Cooking Instructions:

1. Cut each of the ingredients in half Preheat oven to 325ºF.

2. Fill a 9x11 baking dish halfway with warm water, then place a greased 12-count silicone egg tray overtop.

3. Divide toppings of choice and cheese among egg cups, then fill the rest of the way full with eggs or egg whites.

4. Bake in the oven for about 60 minutes or until eggs are set. Remove egg bites from molds once cool and serve and enjoy!

Sweet Potato Meal Prep Breakfast Bowls

Preparation time: 15 minutes

Cooking time: 30 minutes

Overall time: 45 minutes

Serves: 2 to 4 people

Recipe Ingredients:

- 1 tbsp. of olive oil
- 4 cups of sweet potatoes cut into 1/2-inch cubes
- 2 tsp. of chili powder
- ¼ tsp. of salt
- ½ cup of water
- 2 bell peppers diced
- 1 cup of mushrooms sliced
- 4 eggs
- ¼ cup of milk
- ¼ tsp. of salt
- ½ tsp. of chili powder

Cooking Instructions:

1. In a large bowl, toss the olive oil, sweet potatoes, chili powder and salt.

2. Add to a large pan and cook over medium heat for about 10 minutes, stirring occasionally.

3. Add ½ cup water to the pan and cover. Cook for about 10 more minutes, or until sweet potatoes are softened. Portion out into 4 containers.

4. Add additional olive oil to the pan if necessary. Add the bell peppers and mushrooms, and cook for about 5 minutes until softened.

5. While cooking the veggies, beat the eggs with the milk, chili powder and salt. Add to the pan with the veggies.

6. Cook for about 3 more minutes, or until eggs are cooked through. Add to the 4 containers with the sweet potatoes.

7. Store in the fridge for up to 4 days. Heat in the microwave until steaming hot. Serve with salsa and/or avocado.

Egg White Frittata

Preparation time: 5 minutes

Cooking time: 30 minutes

Overall time: 35 minutes

Serves: 2 to 4 people

Recipe Ingredients:

- 2 tablespoons of olive oil
- 1 (500ml) carton of egg whites
- 1 cup of cherry tomatoes, sliced in half
- 1 cup of baby spinach, chopped
- ½ teaspoon of each Salt & pepper

Cooking Instructions:

1. Preheat oven to 400°F. Grease a large shallow round baking dish/cake pan with olive oil, making sure to grease the sides well.

2. Add remaining ingredients, stirring well and gently with a fork.

3. Place baking dish on top of a baking sheet lined with parchment paper just in case a bit of the oil rises above the egg white mixture.

4. Bake in the oven for 30 to 35 minutes until egg whites are firmly set. Remove from oven and slice into 4 to 5 pieces when cooled.

5. Serve immediately and Enjoy!

Carrot Cake Oatmeal Muffin Cups

Preparation time: 15 minutes

Cooking time: 30 minutes

Overall time: 45 minutes

Serves: 4 to 6 people

Recipe Ingredients:

- 2 cups of almond milk
- 2 eggs
- 1/3 cup of maple syrup
- 1 teaspoon of vanilla
- 2 cups of rolled oats
- ½ cup of unsweetened shredded coconut
- 1 carrot, shredded
- ¼ cup of chopped walnuts
- 2 teaspoons of cinnamon
- 1 teaspoon of nutmeg

Cooking Instructions:

1. Preheat oven to 350ºF. In a large bowl, mix together almond milk, eggs, maple syrup and vanilla.

2. In another large bowl, mix together rolled oats, coconut, carrot, walnuts, cinnamon and nutmeg. Fold wet ingredients into dry ingredients.

3. Line muffin tins with cupcake liners. Divide oatmeal mixture among cups, making sure to balance the wet and dry ingredients evenly.

4. Bake in oven for about 30 to 35 minutes. Will keep in the fridge up to 5 days.

Freezer Breakfast Burritos

Preparation time: 15 minutes

Cooking time: 3 minutes

Overall time: 18 minutes

Serves: 8 to 12 people

Recipe Ingredients:

- 12 ounces of reduced-fat sausage
- 8 large eggs
- 1 tablespoon of dry minced onion
- ¼ cup of picante sauce
- 2 cups of shredded Monterey Jack cheese
- 12 flour tortillas, burrito size
- 1 pinch Salt & pepper, to taste

Cooking Instructions:

1. Line baking sheet with parchment paper; set aside. Brown sausage in a non-stick skillet over medium heat.

2. Drain on paper towels; set aside. Wipe grease from skillet leaving a thin layer of oil. Beat eggs with minced onion and picante sauce in a medium bowl.

3. Scramble eggs in skillet until thoroughly cooked. Combine sausage, eggs, and cheese in a large bowl.

4. Add about 2/3 cup of egg mixture to center of tortillas. Wrap by folding sides into middle and rolling tightly.

5. Place burritos on baking sheet and freeze until solid. Wrap individually in paper towels and place in resealable freezer bag. Store in freezer up to 2 months.

6. Reheat burritos by removing from freezer bag, placing on microwave-safe plate, and microwaving for 1 to 2 minutes until heated through.

Strawberry Oatmeal Bars

Preparation time: 5 minutes

Cooking time: 30 minutes

Gross time: 35 minutes

Serves: 6 to 8 people

Recipe Ingredients:

- 1 cup of quick or rolled oats
- ½ cup of spelt, white, or oat flour
- ¼ teaspoon of each: cinnamon, salt, and baking powder
- 1/3 cup of sugar, unrefined if desired
- 1/3 cup of oil
- 2 cups of diced strawberries
- 1 ½ teaspoon of cornstarch or arrowroot
- 1 tablespoon of sweetener of choice, or pinch uncut stevia

Cooking Instructions:

1. Preheat oven to 350ºF. Line an 8×8 pan with parchment. In a large bowl, stir together the oats, flour, cinnamon, salt, baking powder, and sugar.

2. Stir in the oil, then very firmly press 2/3 of the dough into the prepared pan, reserving the remaining dough.

3. In a separate bowl, stir berries, starch, and 1 tablespoon of sweetener. Press this on top of the dough in the pan, then sprinkle the reserved dough on top.

4. Press down very firmly again. Bake 35 minutes on the center rack. Let cool, then refrigerate at least 1 hour before cutting, as they firm up considerably.

5. Eat plain, or top with melted coconut butter, frosting, or a basic powdered sugar glaze.

Flourless Blender Muffins

Preparation time: 5 minutes

Cooking time: 15 minutes

Overall time: 20 minutes

Serves: 3 to 5 people

Recipe Ingredients:

- ½ cup of quick oats or quinoa flakes
- ¾ teaspoon of baking powder
- ¼ teaspoon of salt
- 1/8 teaspoon of baking soda
- ½ cup of mashed overripe banana
- 1 can of white beans, or 250g cooked beans
- ¼ cup of peanut butter or allergy-friendly sub
- ¼ cup of pure maple syrup or honey (For a sugar-free version, click here)
- 2 teaspoons of pure vanilla extract
- Optional handful mini chocolate chips, crushed walnuts, shredded coconut, pinch cinnamon, etc.

Cooking Instructions:

1. Preheat the oven to 350 F and line 8-9 muffin cups. Drain the beans and rinse extremely well, then pat dry.

2. It is important because it gets rid of any bean taste. Blend all ingredients until smooth in a blender or high-quality food processor.

3. Pour into the muffin cups – don't overfill or they will rise and then sink in the centers. Bake for about 20 minutes.

4. They will look underdone – let sit 20 minutes and they will firm up. These muffins are supposed to be fudgy, not fluffy and flour-y like traditional muffins.

5. Not everyone will be a fan of the texture, but if you like my black bean brownies, then you will probably like these as well! Serve and Enjoy!

6. Muffins last for 3 to 4 days refrigerated or 2 to 3 weeks frozen.

Lentil Soup

Preparation time: 5 minutes

Cooking time: 20 minutes

Total Time: 25 minutes

Serves: 3 to 5 people

Recipe Ingredients:

- ½ of a large onion, diced
- 1 ½ tablespoons of oil (can be omitted for fat free)
- ¼ cup of chopped celery
- 14 ounces of chopped tomatoes
- 14 ounces of vegetable broth
- 1 ½ cups of cooked or canned lentils
- ¼ cup of chopped carrots
- ¼ cup of uncooked pearl barley or rice
- 1 teaspoon of salt
- ½ teaspoon of dried rosemary
- Optional pepper to taste

Cooking Instructions:

1. Either sauté onion in oil or just combine it with the celery, tomatoes, and broth.

2. Bring to a boil over medium-high heat. Pulverize. Then add all remaining ingredients, lower to a simmer, and cover.

3. Simmer for about 25 minutes or until carrots and barley are tender. Taste, and add additional seasonings if desired.

4. Serve immediately and Enjoy!

Healthy Banana Bread

Preparation time: 10 minutes

Cooking time: 40 minutes

Overall time: 50 minutes

Serves: 6 to 8 people

Recipe Ingredients:

- 2 cups of white, spelt, or oat flour (240g)
- 1 teaspoon of baking soda
- ¾ teaspoon of baking powder
- ¾ teaspoon of salt
- Optional ½ teaspoon of cinnamon
- Optional ½ cup of mini chocolate chips
- 1 ½ cup of mashed, overripe banana (360g)
- ½ cup of yogurt, such as almond milk yogurt
- ½ cup of pure maple syrup, honey, or agave
- 2 tablespoons any sweetener of choice OR 1/16 tsp uncut stevia
- 1/3 cup of oil OR milk of choice
- 2 teaspoons of pure vanilla extract

Cooking Instructions:

1. Preheat oven to 350°F. Grease a 9×5 loaf pan, or line with parchment.

2. Combine dry ingredients in a bowl. Whisk liquid ingredients in a separate bowl. Pour wet into dry, and stir to form a batter. Smooth into the prepared pan.

3. If desired, press some chocolate chips into the top. Bake on the center rack for about 40 minutes.

4. Do not open the oven door but turn off the heat and let sit in the closed oven 10 additional minutes.

5. If your bread is still undercooked at this time, simply turn the oven back on and continue baking.

6. Check every 5 minutes, until a toothpick inserted into the center comes out clean. Let cool completely.

7. Cover and refrigerate overnight. Taste and texture are much better the second day Leftovers can be sliced and frozen for up to a month.

Chia Pudding

Preparation time: 5 minutes

Cooking time: 5 minutes

Gross time: 10 minutes

Serves: 1 to 3 people

Recipe Ingredients:

- 1 cup of milk of choice or cashew cream
- ¼ cup of chia seeds
- ¼ teaspoon of pure vanilla extract
- Sweetener of choice, as desired
- Scant 1/8 teaspoon of salt

Cooking Instructions:

1. Whisk all ingredients in a container. If desired, you can blend everything together now, which will result in a smoother consistency the next day.

2. Cover, shake, then refrigerate overnight. The next day, it will be nice and thick. The pudding will keep 4 to 5 days refrigerated,

3. Feel free to make a larger batch and portion into individual containers.

Oatmeal Cupcakes

Preparation time: 5 minutes

Cooking time: 20 minutes

Gross time: 25 minutes

Serves: 10 to 12 people

Recipe Ingredients:

- 5 cups of rolled oats
- 2 ½ cups of over-ripe mashed banana
- 1 teaspoon of salt
- 5 tablespoons of pure maple syrup, agave, or honey OR stevia equivalent amount
- 2/3 cup of mini chocolate chips, optional
- 2 1/3 cups of water - Increase to 2 2/3 cups if using stevia
- ¼ cup + 1 tablespoon of coconut or veg oil
- 2 ½ teaspoon of pure vanilla extract
- Optional add-ins: cinnamon, shredded coconut, chopped walnuts, ground flax or chia, wheat germ, raisins, dried fruit, etc.

Cooking Instructions:

1. Preheat oven to 380ºF, and line 24 to 25 cupcake tins.

2. In a large mixing bowl, combine all dry ingredients and stir very well. In a separate bowl, combine and stir all wet ingredients (including banana).

3. Mix wet into dry, then pour into the cupcake liners and bake 21 minutes. I also like to then broil for 1-2 minutes, but it's optional.

4. These oatmeal cakes can be eaten right away, or they can be frozen and reheated for an instant breakfast on a busy day.

Overnight Oats

Preparation time: 5 minutes

Cooking time: 5 minutes

Overall time: 5 minutes

Serves: 1 to 3 people

Recipe Ingredients:

- ½ cup of rolled oats or quick oats
- ½ cup of milk of choice
- ½ cup of yogurt or additional milk of choice
- Sweetener of choice, as desired
- 1/8 teaspoon of salt
- Optional ½ cup of fruit of choice
- Optional 1 to2 tablespoon of nut butter
- Optional 1 tablespoon chia seeds, or add-ins of choice

Cooking Instructions:

1. Combine all ingredients in a lidded container or mason jar.

2. Shake well, then refrigerate overnight. The next morning, simply stir and enjoy!

Banana Egg Pancakes

Preparation time: 5 minutes

Cooking time: 20 minutes

Overall time: 25 minutes

Serves: 2 to 4 people

Recipe Ingredients:

- 8 eggs
- 4 bananas
- Fruit and/or nuts to serve on the side
- Maple syrup to serve on the side (optional)

Cooking Instructions:

1. Mash bananas together in a large bowl then whisk in eggs.

2. Heat butter in a large frying pan over medium heat and add about ¼ cup of pancake batter at a time, cooking for 3 to 4 minutes per side until fully cooked.

3. Add pancakes to meal prep bowls along with fruit and maple syrup on the side. Will keep in fridge up to 5 days.

4. Stack pancakes in between wax paper and store in a resealable plastic bag. Microwave for about 1 to 2 minutes to reheat. Makes 16-20 mini pancakes.

Breakfast Sandwiches

Preparation time: 15 minutes

Cooking time: 15 minutes

Overall time: 30 minutes

Serves: 10 to 12 people

Recipe Ingredients:

- 12 eggs
- ¼ cup of whole milk
- 1 ½ tsp. of salt
- 6 slices of bacon
- A few handfuls of spinach
- 12 English muffins
- Cheese (optional)
- Butter (optional)

Cooking Instructions:

1. Preheat oven to 300°F. Generously oil a rimmed half sheet pan. Whisk the eggs, milk, and salt.

2. Cut the bacon into small pieces. Fry in a heavy skillet until crispy. Add the spinach and stir until wilted.

3. Using tongs, let excess fat drip off for a few seconds before adding your bacon and spinach to the egg mixture.

4. Pour the egg mixture into the oiled half sheet pan (13″ x 18″). Bake for about 15 minutes, until just set.

5. Remove, cool, and cut into rounds using a wide mason jar lid or round cookie cutter.

6. Spread English muffins with butter (optional) and place an egg round on each one. Add cheese, wrap in foil, and voila.

7. Refrigerate (4 to 5 days) or freeze (no limit, lol). To reheat, you can use the oven, microwave, toaster oven, or some combination of all!

POULTRY RECIPES

Baked Buffalo Chicken Casserole

Preparation time: 10 minutes

Cooking time: 45 minutes

Gross time: 55 minutes

Serves: 2 to 4 people

Recipe Ingredients:

- 1 lb. of boneless skinless chicken breast cooked & shredded
- 425 grams of cauliflower riced
- 1 small onion diced
- ½ cup of carrots diced
- ½ clove of garlic minced
- 1 tbsp. of ghee
- ¼ tsp. of black pepper
- ½ - ¾ cup of buffalo sauce
- 1/2 cup of egg whites
- Ranch dressing if desired
- Chives if desired

Cooking Instructions:

1. Preheat oven to 400°F. Line a baking pan with parchment paper Add ghee, onion, carrots, celery and garlic to a skillet

2. Sauté until onion is translucent and softened. Add cauliflower rice, shredded chicken, Sautéed veggies, egg whites and buffalo sauce to a bowl.

3. Mix well. Pour into lined baking pan. Bake covered for 25 minutes. Remove cover and bake an additional 20 to 25 minutes or until set.

4. Top with ranch and chives, if desired. Divide between meal prep containers

Bacon Wrapped Chicken

Preparation time: 5 minutes

Cooking time: 15 minutes

Overall time: 20 minutes

Serves: 2 to 4 people

Recipe Ingredients:

- 4 (4 ounces) of chicken breast
- 8 slices of paleo friendly bacon
- 1 teaspoon of paprika
- 1 teaspoon of thyme
- 1 teaspoon of onion powder
- Salt & pepper as desired

Cooking Instructions:

1. Heat a large oven safe skillet on the stove to medium heat.

2. While skillet heats, wrap 2 slices of bacon around each chicken breast. If your chicken breast is very thick, smooth it thinner with a mallet first.

3. You want each breast to be evenly sized all the way through so the chicken and bacon cook perfectly. Place each wrapped chicken breast on the preheated skillet.

4. Cook for about 3 to 4 minutes on each side. While the chicken is cooking preheat the oven to 350°F.

5. Place the skillet in the oven. Bake at 350°F for about 10 minutes. This makes the bacon extra crispy.

6. Serve with your favorite vegetable and a side of sweet potato fries.

Hawaiian Pizza Chicken

Preparation time: 15 minutes

Cooking time: 24 minutes

Overall time: 39 minutes

Serves: 4 people

Recipe Ingredients:

- 4 medium chicken breasts
- 1 tablespoon of Italian seasoning
- Salt & pepper to taste
- ¾ cup of pizza sauce
- 1 cup of shredded mozzarella cheese
- ½ cup of Canadian bacon
- ½ cup of pineapple diced
- Parmesan & red pepper flakes for garnish, optional
- 2 cups of broccoli steamed

Cooking Instructions:

1. Preheat oven to 425ºF. Add chicken breasts to a baking dish, and season both sides with sea salt, pepper, and Italian seasoning.

2. Bake chicken for about 18 minutes, until it's slightly undercooked. Top chicken breasts with pizza sauce, sliced or shredded mozzarella, ham and pineapple.

3. Return to oven to bake for another 10 to 12 minutes, until the cheese is starting to brown and bubble. Serve with steamed broccoli.

Thai Basil Chicken

Preparation time: 10 minutes

Cooking time: 10 minutes

Gross time: 20 minutes

Serves: 2 to 4 people

Recipe Ingredients:

- 1.5 lb. of chicken breast
- 3 tablespoons of sesame oil
- ¼ cup of Thai shallots
- 2 tablespoons of minced garlic
- 2 to 3 Thai bird chilis
- ½ cup of coconut aminos
- 3 tablespoons of honey
- 1 to 2 tablespoons of fish sauce
- ¼ cup of chicken broth
- 1 teaspoon of arrowroot
- 2 cups of fresh Thai basil

Cooking Instructions:

1. Add sesame oil to a skillet on high heat. Add shallots, garlic, and chilis, and stir fry for about 2 minutes to soften and infuse the oil with their flavors.

2. Add the chicken, and break up, continuing to stir fry on high heat. Add the coconut aminos, honey, and fish sauce, and stir to combine.

3. Add arrowroot powder to the chicken broth and stir. When most of the liquid has evaporated, push the chicken to the edge of the pan.

4. Deglaze the pan with the chicken broth meaning, scrape the flavorful coating off the bottom of the pan.

5. Stir quickly to mix together the sauce, and then coat the chicken with the sauce. Add the whole basil leaves, and stir fry for about 30 seconds to allow them to wilt.

6. Serve over rice or other whole grain, with steamed vegetables, if desired.

Chili Lime Chicken and Rice

Preparation time: 10 minutes

Cooking time: 20 minutes

Gross time 30 minutes

Serves: 2 to 4 people

Recipe Ingredients:

- 1 lb. of boneless skinless chicken breasts
- 2 cups of sliced bell peppers optional
- 4 cups of cooked rice of choice

For the chicken marinade:

- 2 tbsp. of fresh lime juice or juice of 1 lime
- 2 tsp. of lime zest or zest of 1 lime
- 2 to 3 cloves of garlic minced or crush
- ¼ cup of cilantro minced
- 4 tbsp. of oil
- 1 tbsp. of brown sugar
- 2 tsp. of chili powder
- ½ tsp. of cumin powder optional
- 1 tsp. of salt
- ¼ tsp. of black pepper
- 4 meal-prep containers

Cooking Instructions:

1. In a large bowl, whisk together all the ingredients for the marinade. Add the chicken and mix until fully coated.

2. Preheat grill or skillet to medium-high, grease with a little oil. Transfer chicken to pan and discard remaining marinade.

3. Grill chicken for about 5 to 8 minutes on each side or until cooked through. Cool chicken for 5 minutes then slice.

4. Remove chicken from the pan and immediately add sliced bell peppers to the same pan. Cook for about 3 to 4 minutes or until charred.

5. Let everything come to room temperature before assembling the meal prep boxes. To assemble, Add 1 cup of cooked rice into 4 meal prep containers.

6. Divide chicken and bell peppers into each box. Shut the lid and refrigerate for up to four days.

Greek Rice & Turkey

Preparation time: 10 minutes

Cooking time: 15 minutes

Gross time: 25 minutes

Serves: 2 to 4 people

Recipe Ingredients:

- 1 lb. of ground turkey breast
- 2 cups of brown rice cooked
- ¼ cup of chicken broth
- 1 tablespoon of olive oil
- 1 tablespoon of lemon juice
- ¼ cup of black olives
- ¼ cup of sun-dried tomatoes, roughly chopped not packed in oil
- 1 tablespoon of oregano
- 1 tablespoon of parsley
- Salt & pepper
- 1 cup of cucumber slices
- Fresh lemon slices

Cooking Instructions:

1. Place the turkey in a large skillet with extra virgin olive oil, salt, pepper, oregano and garlic and bring to a medium heat.

2. Breakup the meat with a wooden spoon while the meat browns, about 5 minutes. Add the chicken broth and lemon juice.

3. Let the juices simmer for about 2 to 3 minutes with the meat. Add the black olives, chopped sun-dried tomatoes and parsley to the skillet.

4. Stir to combine and cook another 5 minutes. Divide the meat mixture into 4 meal prep containers paired with brown rice, cucumber slices and lemons.

Baked Eggs

Preparation time: 10 minutes

Cooking time: 15 minutes

Gross time: 25 minutes

Serves: 8 to 12 people

Recipe Ingredients:

- 12 eggs
- Salt & pepper

Optional:

- Ham slices
- Turkey slices
- Cooked bacon

Cooking Instructions:

1. Heat oven to 350°F and spray a standard-sized muffin tin with spray oil.

2. Carefully break the eggs right into the muffin tin, or into a small bowl, then pour into the muffin tin.

3. Season with salt and pepper. Bake for about 15 for 18 minutes, until eggs are done to your liking.

4. Store in an airtight container in the fridge for up to 4 days. Reheat in the microwave or enjoy cold!

Egg Muffin Cups

Preparation time: 10 minutes

Cooking time: 20 minutes

Gross time: 30 minutes

Serves: 4 to 6 people

Recipe Ingredients:

- ½ dozen of eggs
- Coconut oil for the muffin tin

Choose from any of the following:

- Kale, chopped
- Baby spinach, chopped
- Tomatoes, diced
- Onions, finely chopped
- Red bell peppers, finely chopped
- Green peppers, finely chopped
- Mushrooms, finely chopped
- Goat cheese, crumbled
- Basil, finely chopped
- Mozzarella cheese, shredded
- Salt and pepper to taste, (other seasonings too like oregano or garlic powder!)
- Fire roasted salsa, for topping the eggs!

Cooking Instructions:

1. Preheat oven to 350°F. Spray a nonstick muffin tin with nonstick cooking spray or melted coconut oil. Set aside.

2. Whisk the eggs in a bowl. Place 2-3 items from the list above into each tin. You can customize each muffin cup however you want.

3. Pour the egg mixture on top, leaving ¼ "from the top. Bake for about 20 minutes, or until a toothpick comes out clean for each frittata.

4. Remove from oven and use a knife to go around the edges and pop out the egg cups.

5. To reheat, simply place one egg muffin in the microwave for about 35 to 45 seconds on High until it is warm. Enjoy!

Ground Turkey Stir Fry

Preparation time: 10 minutes

Cooking time: 15 minutes

Gross time: 25 minutes

Serves: 3 to 5 people

Recipe Ingredients:

Stir Fry Sauce:

- ¼ cup of soy sauce
- ½ tablespoon of toasted sesame oil
- ½ tablespoon of brown sugar
- 1 pinch red pepper flakes (optional)
- 1 tablespoon of water

Stir Fry:

- 2 bell peppers
- 4 green onions
- 2 ounces of spinach, two large handfuls
- 2 tablespoons of cooking oil of choice
- 2 cloves of garlic, minced
- 19 ounces of ground turkey

For Serving:

- ¼ cup of chopped peanuts
- 2.5 cups of cooked brown rice

Cooking Instructions:

1. Stir together the soy sauce, toasted sesame oil, brown sugar, red pepper, and water until the sugar is dissolved. Set the sauce aside.

2. Dice the bell peppers and slice the green onions. Heat the cooking oil in a very large skillet over medium heat. Once hot, add the ground turkey and minced garlic.

3. Stir and cook until the turkey is cooked through and no water is left pooling on the bottom of the skillet for about 8 to 10 minutes.

4. Once the turkey is cooked and the moisture has evaporated, add the bell pepper and green onions to the skillet.

5. Stir and cook for about 2 minutes more, then add the spinach and continue to cook just until it is about half wilted (1-2 minutes). Pour the stir fry sauce into the skillet.

6. Continue to stir and cook the turkey and vegetables until everything is coated in sauce and the spinach is fully wilted (about 2 minutes more).

7. Serve about 1 cup of the stir fry mixture with 1/2 cup rice and a sprinkle of chopped peanuts over top.

Korean Turkey

Preparation time: 20 minutes

Cooking time: 20 minutes

Overall time: 40 minutes

Serves: 2 to 4 people

Recipe Ingredients:

- 1 tbsp. of olive oil
- ¾ cup of uncooked rice
- 1 head broccoli chopped into florets

Turkey:

- ¾ pound of lean ground turkey
- 4 cloves of garlic minced
- 1 tbsp. of ginger finely chopped

Sauce:

- 3 tbsp. of honey
- 3 tbsp. of soy sauce (reduced sodium)
- 1 ½ tsp. of sesame oil
- ¼ tsp. of red pepper flakes
- 1/8 tsp. of pepper

Garnish:

- Green onions (optional)

Cooking Instructions:

1. Cook rice and portion out into four 2-cup capacity meal prep containers and allow to cool. Shake up all sauce ingredients and set aside.

2. Heat oil in a large pan over medium heat. Add the broccoli and cook for about 6 minutes, until slightly softened.

3. Remove it from heat and divide between the meal prep containers. Add turkey to pan.

4. Cook, breaking it up with a spatula, for about 5 to 8 minutes, until completely cooked through and no longer pink.

5. Make a space in the middle of the pan. Add the garlic and ginger and cook for 1 minute, stirring up a bit.

6. Give the sauce a shake up and pour over the ground turkey and garlic/ginger. Stir until everything is mixed through, about 1-2 minutes.

7. Remove from heat. Divide turkey/sauce mixture between the meal prep containers. Sprinkle with green onions if desired.

Fiesta Chicken Rice

Preparation time: 10 minutes

Cooking time: 20 minutes

Overall time: 30 minutes

Serves: 2 to 4 people

Recipe Ingredients:

- 1 tablespoon of olive oil
- 1 pound of chicken breasts (about 3-4 medium-sized breasts)
- 1 tablespoon of chili powder
- 1 teaspoon of salt
- 1 teaspoon of garlic powder
- 1 teaspoon of cumin
- ½ cup of corn
- 2 small red onions, sliced
- 1 red pepper, diced
- 1 green pepper, diced
- 1 yellow pepper, diced
- ¾ cup of fresh salsa
- 1/3 cup of cilantro, chopped
- ¼ cup of feta cheese (optional, divided)

Rice:

- 1 cup of dry brown rice
- 2 cups of water
- 1 teaspoon of butter

Cooking Instructions:

1. Get rice cooking in a rice cooker while you prep ingredients.

2. In a large frying pan, heat olive oil over med-high heat. Add chicken and stir fry for 2-3 min until lightly cooked.

3. Add chili powder, cumin and garlic powder, then toss to coat and continue cooking another 5 minutes.

4. Add red onion, corn and bell peppers, sautéing for about 2 to 3 minutes. Add cooked brown rice and salsa, tossing to coat.

5. Cook for about 5 minutes. Mix in cilantro and remove from heat. Sprinkle with feta cheese if desired and serve!

Sesame Chicken Pasta Salad

Preparation time: 15 minutes

Cooking time: 25 minutes

Overall time40 minutes

Serves: 2 to 4 people

Recipe Ingredients:

Pasta:

- 2 cups of 4.6 ounces uncooked pasta

Chicken:

- 2 large chicken breasts
- 1 tbsp. of sesame oil
- 1 tbsp. of soy sauce
- Sesame Vinaigrette
- 2 tbsp. of olive oil
- 2 tbsp. of rice vinegar
- 1.5 tbsp. of honey
- 1.5 tbsp. of sesame oil
- ¾ tsp. of soy sauce
- 1 clove of garlic optional
- 1/8 teaspoon of salt

Other:

- 10-ounce bag of Mann's Power Blend
- Sesame seeds
- Green onions

Cooking Instructions:

1. Cook the pasta and heat oven to 425°F.

2. Toss the chicken breasts in the sesame oil and soy sauce and bake in a small baking dish for about 10 minutes.

3. Flip and return to the oven for about 10 to 15 minutes, until cooked through. Allow to rest for about 5 minutes on a cutting board before slicing into strips.

4. Shake together all vinaigrette ingredients, and toss in a large bowl with the cooked chicken, pasta, and Mann's Power Blend, until completely coated.

5. Divide amongst 4 storage containers, sprinkle with sesame seeds and green onions, and refrigerate.

Garlic Marinated Chicken

Preparation time: 45 minutes

Cooking time: 15 minutes

Overall time: 1 hour

Serves: 2 to 4 people

Recipe Ingredients:

- ¼ cup of olive oil
- ¼ cup of lemon juice
- 3 cloves of garlic, minced
- ½ tablespoon of dried oregano
- ½ teaspoon of salt
- Freshly cracked pepper
- 1.5 pounds of boneless skinless chicken breasts

Cooking Instructions:

1. Add the olive oil, lemon juice, garlic, oregano, salt, and pepper to a large zip top bag, or a large shallow dish.

2. Close the bag and massage to combine the ingredients, or stir the ingredients in the dish until combined.

3. Filet each chicken breast into two thinner pieces. Place the pieces in the bag or dish, making sure the chicken pieces are completely covered in marinade.

4. Marinate the chicken for about 30 minutes up to 8 hours, turning occasionally to maximize the chicken's contact with the marinade.

5. When ready to cook, heat a large skillet over medium flame. Transfer the chicken from the marinade to the hot skillet.

6. Cook on each side until well browned and cooked through for about 5 to 7 minutes each side, depending on the size of the pieces.

7. Discard the excess marinade. Transfer the cooked chicken from the skillet to a cutting board and let rest for five minutes before slicing and serving.

8. Serve immediately and Enjoy!

Cajun-Honey Chicken Bowls

Preparation time: 10 minutes

Cook time: 30 minutes

Gross time: 40 minutes

Serves: 2 to 4 people

Recipe Ingredients:

- 2 lb. boneless, skinless chicken breasts sliced into strips
- 1 red bell pepper seeded and sliced
- 1 jalapeño pepper seeded and sliced
- Orange slices cut in half
- Lime wedges for garnish, optional
- 2 green onions sliced, for garnish, optional
- Fresh parsley minced, for garnish, optional
- 1/3 cup of honey
- 1/3 cup of orange juice (fresh is best if possible)
- 2 tbsp. of brown sugar
- 3 tbsp. of coarse Dijon mustard
- 1 tbsp. of yellow mustard
- ¾ tbsp. of Cajun seasoning
- 2 cloves of garlic minced
- ½ tsp. of salt
- ¼ tsp. of pepper

Cooking Instructions:

1. Trim chicken breasts of fat, and slice into strips to resemble chicken tenders.

2. Add marinade ingredients to a zip-top plastic bag and whisk to combine. Add chicken to bag, and seal, pressing out any excess air.

3. Smoosh the bag around a bit to make sure all the chicken pieces are coated in the marinade. Place bag on a plate and refrigerate up to 8 hours.

4. Pour entire contents of the bag into a large skillet and heat over MED-HIGH heat until the mixture comes to a bubble.

5. Reduce heat to MED-LOW and simmer, uncovered, for about 25 to 30 minutes, until most of the liquid cooks off, leaving a loose glaze.

6. The last 5 minutes or so, add in the sliced bell pepper, jalapeño and orange slices and let them cook in the glaze. Remove chicken, veggies and oranges to a plate.

7. Serve over rice, quinoa, or as is for a low carb option. If desired, garnish with sliced green onions, minced parsley, and a lime wedge.

Pesto Chicken

Preparation time: 20 minutes

Cooking time: 20 minutes

Overall time: 40 minutes

Serves: 2 to 4 people

Recipe Ingredients:

- 4 medium chicken breasts
- 1 whole30 pesto
- ½ cup of sundried tomatoes chopped (not packed in oil)
- ½ cup of black olives chopped
- 1 lb. of asparagus
- 1 cup of cherry tomatoes sliced
- 2 tablespoons of walnuts, chopped for garnish, optional
- Whole30 Pesto
- 5 cups of loosely packed basil
- ¼ cup of olive oil
- 2 tablespoons of lemon juice
- ¼ cup of walnuts
- 1 clove of garlic grated
- ¼ teaspoon of salt

Cooking Instructions:

1. Preheat oven to 425°F. Prepare pesto by adding the basil to a food processor bowl, and processing until greens are chopped finely.

2. Add the lemon juice, walnuts and sea salt, and begin to process. While the mixture is chopping, slowly drizzle the olive oil into the food processor bowl.

3. Add the grated garlic and mix to combine. Take each chicken breast, and pound it flat.

4. Take each flattened breast, and add ¼ of the pesto mixture, and 2 tablespoons each sundried tomatoes and olives.

5. Roll up the chicken breasts, and place into a baking dish. Bake the chicken for about 20 to 24 minutes, until the juices run clear and the chicken is fully baked.

6. Sauté asparagus, and serve with sliced chicken and cherry tomatoes. Garnish with chopped walnuts for a delicious nutty flavor and texture.

Hawaiian Chicken Teriyaki Skewer

Preparation time: 40 minutes

Cooking time: 15 minutes

Overall time: 55 minutes

Serves: 8 to 10 people

Recipe Ingredients:

- ½ cup of coconut aminos
- ½ cup of rice wine vinegar
- 1/3 cup of pineapple juice
- 3 tablespoons of honey
- 2 cloves of garlic minced
- 2 teaspoons of fresh grated ginger
- ½ teaspoon of salt
- ¼ teaspoon of black pepper
- 2.5 lb. of skinless chicken breast cut into bite sized pieces
- 1 green bell pepper cut into bite sized pieces
- 1 orange bell pepper cut into bite sized pieces
- Avocado oil as needed for grill

Cooking Instructions:

1. In a medium bowl, whisk together coconut aminos, rice vinegar, pineapple juice, honey, garlic, ginger, salt, and pepper.

2. Reserve about 1/3 cup of marinade. Combine remaining marinade with chicken, making sure chicken is well coated.

3. Cover with plastic wrap and chill in the fridge for 30 minutes, no longer than 1 hour. If using wooden skewers, soak skewers in water for at least 30 minutes.

4. Preheat the grill for high heat. Thread chicken, onion, and bell peppers onto soaked wooden skewers. Brush oil over grill grates.

5. Place assembled chicken skewers once grill registers 400ºF. Brush other side of chicken skewers with oil.

6. Cook for about 5 to 7 minutes on each side until chicken is cooked through and registers at least 165ºF on an instant read kitchen thermometer.

7. Warm up reserved marinade. Brush onto cooked chicken skewers. Serve warm.

Pizza Chicken

Preparation time: 10 minutes

Cooking time: 16 minutes

Overall time: 26 minutes

Serves: 2 to 4 people

Recipe Ingredients:

- 1 lb. of chicken breast
- ½ cup of pizza sauce
- 1 ½ tablespoons of pizza seasoning
- 4 ounces of mozzarella cheese
- 2 ounces of pepperoni
- 2 cups of broccoli steamed

Cooking Instructions:

1. Preheat oven to 375°F. Place chicken on a baking sheet and top with pizza sauce and pizza seasoning.

2. Bake for about 8 to 10 minutes Remove from the oven and top chicken with mozzarella cheese and additional seasoning, if desired.

3. Bake for an additional 6 minutes. Remove from the oven and add pepperoni, if using Return to the oven until chicken is done cooking.

4. Serve with steamed broccoli

Healthy Chicken and Veggies

Preparation time: 10 minutes

Cooking time 20 minutes

Overall time: 30 minutes

Serves: 2 to 4 people

Recipe Ingredients:

- 2 medium chicken breasts boneless skinless cut into 1/2 inch pieces
- 1 cup of broccoli florets frozen or fresh
- 1 small red onion chopped
- 1 cup of grape or plum tomatoes
- 1 medium zucchini chopped
- 2 cloves of garlic minced
- 1 tbsp. of Italian seasoning
- 1 tsp. of salt
- ½ tsp. of black pepper optional
- ½ tsp. of red pepper flakes optional
- ½ tsp. of paprika
- 2 tbsp. of olive oil
- 2 to 4 cups of cooked rice of choice optional
- 4 meal prep containers

Cooking Instructions:

1. Pre-heat oven to 450°F. Line a baking sheet with aluminum foil and set aside.

2. Place the chicken and veggies in the baking dish. Sprinkle all the spices and garlic evenly over the chicken and veggies. Drizzle with the olive oil.

3. Bake for about 15 to 20 minutes or until the veggies are charred and chicken is tender.

4. Place ½ or 1 cup of cooked rice of choice into 4 individual meal prep containers. Divide chicken and veggies evenly on top of the rice.

5. Cover and store in the fridge for up to 5 days or freezer up to 2 months.

Shrimp Taco

Preparation time: 10 minutes

Cooking time: 15 minutes

Overall time: 25 minutes

Serves: 2 to 4 people

Recipe Ingredients:

Spicy Shrimp:

- 20 medium shrimp peeled and deveined
- 1 tbsp. of olive oil
- 1 clove of garlic minced
- ½ tsp. of ground cumin
- ½ tsp. of chili powder
- ¼ tsp. of onion powder optional
- ¼ tsp. of kosher salt

For the assembly:

- 2 cups of cooked brown rice
- 1 cup of black beans drained and rinsed
- 1 cup of corn drained and rinsed
- 1 cup of tomatoes diced
- ½ cup of cheddar cheese
- 2 tbsp. of cilantro minced
- 1 lime cut into 4 slices
- 4 meal prep containers

Cooking Instructions:

1. In a medium bowl whisk together olive oil, garlic, cumin, chili and onion powders, and salt.

2. Add in shrimp and toss to coat completely. Cover and refrigerate for at least 10 minutes or up to 24 hours.

3. Heat a large heavy-duty or cast-iron skillet on high heat for about 2 minutes. Add the olive oil and shrimp.

4. Cook shrimp in a skillet on medium-high heat until pink and cooked through, for about 5 minutes. Divide brown rice into 4 meal prep containers (½ cup each).

5. Top with 5 shrimps, a scoop of black beans, corn, tomatoes, a sprinkle of cheese, cilantro and a slice of lime.

6. Cover and refrigerate for a max of 4 days. Heat bowls in the microwave for about 2 minutes or until heated thoroughly.

7. Drizzle with lime juice and top with salsa, sour-cream or guacamole if desired.

Teriyaki Chicken and Broccoli

Preparation time: 5 minutes

Cooking time: 12 minutes

Overall time: 17 minutes

Serves: 2 to 4 people

Recipe Ingredients:

- 1 lb. of boneless skinless chicken breasts, cut into bite-sized pieces
- Salt and pepper
- 1 tbsp. of oil
- 2 cups of broccoli florets
- 1 bell pepper sliced into strips
- Sesame seeds for garnish optional
- 2 cups of cooked brown rice
- 4 meal prep containers

For the teriyaki sauce:

- ¼ cup of light soy sauce or 2 tablespoons dark soy
- 2 tbsp. of honey
- 2 tbsp. of rice wine vinegar
- 1 tbsp. of cornstarch
- 1 clove of garlic peeled and minced
- ½ tsp. of sesame oil optional
- ¼ tsp. of ground ginger optional

Cooking Instructions:

1. Heat a large pan to medium-high heat. Add chicken, season with salt and pepper and cook until no longer pink for about 2 to 3 minutes.

2. Whisk all the ingredients for the teriyaki sauce in a small bowl. Add the teriyaki sauce to chicken and cook for about 4 to 5 minutes or until sauce is thick.

3. Remove chicken from heat. Add the broccoli florets and bell pepper to the same pan. Stir fry for 2-3 minutes or until the bell pepper is slightly softened.

4. Divide the chicken and broccoli into 4 meal prep containers. Add ½ cup of brown rice into each container.

5. Sprinkle with sesame seeds and cover. refrigerate for up to 4 days.

MEAT RECIPES

Pepper Steak

Preparation time: 5 minutes

Cooking time: 15 minutes

Overall time: 20 minutes

Recipe Ingredients:

Main Ingredients:

- 1.5 pounds of sirloin or bottom round steak
- 3 tbsp. of soy sauce
- 1 tsp. of black pepper
- Vegetable oil
- 1 red pepper
- 1 green pepper
- 1 large onion
- 5 to 6 cloves of garlic, minced

Sauce:

- 1 packet of brown gravy mix
- ¼ tsp. of ground ginger (or more to taste)
- ½ tsp. of black pepper
- 1 cup of cold water
- 2 tbsp. of soy sauce

Cooking Instructions:

1. Slice steak into ¼ -inch strips then toss with soy sauce and black pepper.

2. You can cook this strait away or let it marinate up to 8 hours. Chop peppers and onion into 1-inch pieces; set aside.

3. Add just enough vegetable oil to a large skillet to coat the bottom. Heat over high heat until very hot.

4. Add one layer of beef strips to skillet then sauté until nicely browned. Remove from skillet then repeat this process until all beef is browned and set aside.

5. Coat the bottom of the pan with a little more vegetable oil, reduce heat to medium-high then add chopped peppers and onions then sauté for about 3 to 4 minutes.

6. Add minced garlic and continue cooking for 2 minutes. Combine sauce ingredients and mix well.

7. Add sauce and browned beef strips to skillet. Cook and stir until sauce is thickened and peppers are tender.

8. Serve immediately and Enjoy!

Ginger Beef

Preparation time: 20 minutes

Cooking time:10 minutes

Gross time:30 minutes

Serves: 2 to 4 people

Recipe Ingredients:

- 1 lb. skirt steak, sliced thinly
- ½ cup of cornstarch
- ¼ cup of vegetable oil, plus more for frying
- ½ cup of white onion, finely chopped
- 2 cups of carrots, julienned
- 3 cloves of garlic, minced
- 2 tsp. of fresh ginger, grated
- ¼ tsp. of dried red chili flakes
- ½ cup of soy sauce
- ¼ cup of white vinegar
- 2 tbsp. of sesame oil
- ½ tsp. of black pepper
- ½ cup of brown sugar, lightly packed
- 2 tbsp. of sesame seeds

Cooking Instructions:

1. Toss the skirt steak with the corn starch in a large bowl and set aside. Over medium heat, add the vegetable oil and onions to a sauce pan.

2. Sauté for two minutes until onions are translucent. Add the carrots to the onions and sauté for about 3 to 4 minutes until tender.

3. Next, add the garlic, ginger, and chili flakes. Stir into the carrots and onions. Cook for 1 to 2 minutes.

4. Lastly, add the soy sauce, vinegar, sesame oil, black pepper, brown sugar, and sesame seeds. Whisk together.

5. Lower the heat to a simmer and allow the sauce to slightly thicken. In the meantime, bring about 2 to 3 cups of vegetable oil to optimum frying temperature in a deep skillet.

6. Shake the excess corn starch off the beef and fry each piece in batches until crispy. This process takes about 3 to 4 minutes.

7. Drain the fried beef on paper towels. Finally, toss the fried beef with the sauce mixture. Serve immediately.

Balsamic Glazed Roast Beef

Preparation time: 10 minutes

Cooking time: 8 hours 30 minutes

Overall time: 8 hours 40 minutes

Serves: 6 to 8 people

Recipe Ingredients:

- 1 tbsp. of oil
- 3 lb. of Ontario corn fed beef roast such as chuck, round, brisket
- 1 large onion, sliced
- 4 cloves of garlic, chopped
- ½ tsp. of red pepper flakes
- 1 cup of beef broth
- 1/2 cup of balsamic vinegar
- 2 tbsp. of soy sauce (or tamari)
- 2 tbsp. of brown sugar
- 1 tbsp. of Worcestershire sauce
- 1 lb. of baby carrots (optional)
- 1 lb. of mini potatoes or diced potatoes (optional)
- 2 tbsp. of cornstarch + 2 tablespoons water

Cooking Instructions:

1. Heat the oil in a large pan over medium-high heat, add the beef and brown on all sides, for about 20 minutes and set it aside.

2. Add the onions and cook until tender, for about 2 to 3 minutes, before adding the garlic and red pepper flakes and cooking until fragrant, about a minute.

3. Place the beef, onions, broth, balsamic vinegar, soy sauce, brown sugar, Worcestershire sauce, carrots and potatoes in a slow cooker.

4. Cover and cook on low for about 8 to 10 hours or on high for 3-5 hours. Remove the carrots, potatoes and beef and slice or shred the beef.

5. Skim any fat from the cooking juices, place it in a sauce pan, bring to a simmer, add the mixture of the cornstarch and water.

6. Cook until the glaze has thickened a bit. Serve immediately and Enjoy!

Italian Beef and Rice Skillet

Preparation time: 5 minutes

Cooking time: 22 minutes

Overall time: 27 minutes

Serves: 4 to 6 people

Recipe Ingredients:

- ½ onion, diced
- 1 pound of ground beef
- 1 (14.5 ounces) can of Italian diced tomatoes
- 1 ½ cups of frozen mixed veggies (peas and carrots)
- ¾ cup of uncooked white rice
- 2 cups of beef broth
- 1 teaspoon of dried oregano
- 1 teaspoon of garlic salt
- ½ teaspoon of dried basil
- ½ teaspoon of pepper
- 1 ½ cups of shredded mozzarella cheese

Cooking Instructions:

1. Brown the ground beef and onion in a large skillet until no longer pink, drain any excess fat.

2. Return skillet to stove top and add in the tomatoes, mixed veggies, rice, beef broth, oregano, garlic salt, basil and pepper.

3. Stir until combined and bring to a light boil. Reduce heat to a simmer, cover and let cook until rice is tender for about 17 minutes.

4. Fluff rice with fork and top with the mozzarella cheese. Cover with the lid for about 3 minutes to let cheese melt.

5. Sprinkle with parsley if desired. Enjoy!

Steak Burrito Bowl

Preparation time: 10 minutes

Cooking time: 1 hour 10 minutes

Overall time: 1 hour 20 minutes

Serves: 2 to 4 people

Recipe Ingredients:

- 2 lb. flank steak
- 1 tsp. of minced garlic
- ¼ cup of soy sauce
- ¼ cup of olive oil
- ¼ tsp. of cumin
- ¼ tsp. of chili powder
- 2 tbsp. of lime juice
- 2 cups of cooked white rice
- 4 cups of chopped romaine lettuce
- 2 cups of pico de gallo
- 1 (15 oz.) can of black beans
- 1 cup of guacamole
- 1 cups of shredded cheddar cheese
- ½ bunch of chopped cilantro
- 1 lime

Cooking Instructions:

1. Slice steak into ¼ inch strips. In a re-sealable gallon-size Ziploc bag, combine steak, garlic, soy sauce, olive oil, cumin, chili powder, and lime juice.

2. Marinade in the refrigerator for at least 1 hour. Remove steak from the marinade and pan fry over medium heat until it is cooked all the way through.

3. In four bowls, evenly distribute the cooked steak, rice, romaine lettuce, pico de gallo, black beans, guacamole, and shredded cheese.

4. Top with cilantro and lime juice.

Beef Enchiladas

Preparation time: 10 minutes

Cooking time: 30 minutes

Overall time: 40 minutes

Serves: 6 to 8 people

Recipe Ingredients:

For enchiladas

- 1 tablespoon of extra-virgin olive oil
- ½ medium onion, chopped
- 2 cloves of garlic, minced
- 1 pound of ground beef
- 1 teaspoon of chili powder
- 1 teaspoon of cumin
- Kosher salt
- Freshly ground black pepper
- 1(19 ounces) can of enchilada sauce
- 1(15 ounces) can of corn, drained
- 1(15 ounces) can of black beans, drained and rinsed
- 8 flour tortillas
- 2/3 cup of shredded Monterey Jack
- 1/3 cup of shredded cheddar

For topping:

- Quartered grape tomatoes
- Diced avocado
- Finely chopped onion
- Fresh cilantro leaves

Cooking Instructions:

1. Preheat oven to 350°F. In a large skillet over medium heat, heat oil. Add onion and cook until soft, for about 5 minutes.

2. Stir in garlic and cook until fragrant, 1 minute more. Add ground beef and cook until no longer pink, for about 6 minutes.

3. Drain fat. Return beef mixture to skillet and add chili powder and cumin and season with salt and pepper.

4. Stir in enchilada sauce, then remove from heat and stir in corn and black beans. Add a large scoop of meat mixture onto each tortilla and roll up.

5. Place rolled up tortillas side by side in a 9"-x-13" baking dish and top with cheeses. Bake until cheese is melty, for 15 to 18 minutes.

6. Garnish with tomatoes, avocado, onion, and cilantro and serve.

Beef Taco

Preparation time: 5 minutes

Cooking time: 15 minutes

Overall time: 20 minutes

Serves: 2 to 4 people

Recipe Ingredients:

Taco Beef:

- 1 tablespoon of avocado oil
- 1 pound of ground beef
- 1 teaspoon of salt
- ½ tablespoon of chili powder
- 1 teaspoon of cumin
- ½ teaspoon of garlic powder
- ½ teaspoon of onion powder
- 1 teaspoon of paprika
- ¼ teaspoon of cayenne (optional)

Pico de gallo:

- 2 roma tomatoes chopped
- ¼ cup of red onion diced
- 2 tablespoon of lime juice about 1-2 limes
- 3 tablespoons of cilantro chopped
- ½ jalapeno (optional) diced
- 1 clove of garlic minced
- Cilantro lime cauliflower rice
- 1 bag of cauliflower rice fresh or frozen
- 2 tablespoons of cilantro chopped
- ½ jalapeno diced
- 1 lime juiced

Toppings:

- 4 radishes sliced
- 1 avocado
- 1 tablespoon of cilantro chopped
- 1 lime sliced into wedges

Cooking Instructions:

1. Heat oil in a large skillet over medium/high heat and add in the ground beef. Break up the beef into small pieces, leaving no big chunks.

2. Let cook for about 10 to 15 minutes until the excess liquid has evaporated and add in the seasonings.

3. Cook until beef is brown and crispy and set aside, use the same pan that the beef was cooked in and heat to medium.

4. Add in cauliflower rice and jalapeno (if using) and cook until any liquid has evaporated and rice is fluffy.

5. Add in lime and cilantro and season with salt and pepper to taste Combine all the ingredients into a bowl and season to taste with salt and pepper.

6. Place the cooked cauliflower rice in a section, then add the cooked beef, next the pico de gallo.

7. Add additional toppings (leave the avocado until eating) Make sure bowls are completely cool before storing in the fridge

Quick Beef and Broccoli

Preparation time: 15 minutes

Cooking time: 15 minutes

Gross time: 30 minutes

Serves: 2 to 4 people

Recipe Ingredients:

- 1 cup of brown rice
- ¼ cup of reduced sodium soy sauce
- 2 tbsp. of brown sugar, packed
- 3 cloves of garlic, minced
- 1 tbsp. of freshly grated ginger
- 2 tsp. of rice wine vinegar
- 1 tsp. of sesame oil
- 1 tsp. of Sriracha, optional
- 1 tbsp. of olive oil
- 1 lb. of ground beef
- 12 oz. of broccoli florets, cut into 1/2-inch pieces
- 2 green onions, thinly sliced
- 1 tsp. of sesame seeds

Cooking Instructions:

1. In a large saucepan of 2 cups water, cook rice and set it aside.

2. In a small bowl, whisk together soy sauce, brown sugar, garlic, ginger, vinegar, sesame oil and Sriracha. Heat olive oil in a large skillet over medium high heat.

3. Add ground beef and cook until browned, for about 3 to 5 minutes, making sure to crumble the beef as it cooks; drain excess fat.

4. Stir in broccoli, green onions, rice and soy sauce mixture until well combined, allow to simmer until heated through and the broccoli is tender, for about 3-4 minutes.

5. Place mixture into meal prep containers, garnished with sesame seeds, if desired.

Quick Beef Chili

Preparation time: 10 minutes

Cooking time: 45 minutes

Overall time: 55 minutes

Recipe Ingredients:

- 2 lb. beef petite tender steak
- 2 tbsp. of olive oil 1 yellow onion,
- 4 garlic cloves, chopped
- 2 to 3 tsp. of chipotle chile powder, chopped
- 2 tsp. of dried oregano
- 2 tsp. of ground cumin
- 1 (6 ounces) can of tomato paste
- 5 (4.5 ounces) cans of chopped green chiles
- 4 cups of chicken broth
- 1 (14.5 oz.) can of stewed tomatoes
- 2 tbsp. of plain yellow cornmeal
- Toppings: green onions, fried onion rings, sour cream, Cheddar cheese

Cooking Instructions:

1. Sprinkle beef with desired amount of salt and pepper.

2. Cook beef in hot oil in a large, enamel cast-iron Dutch oven over medium-high heat, stirring often, for about 5 to 6 minutes or until browned.

3. Transfer beef to a platter. Add onion to Dutch oven, and cook, stirring often, for about 3 minutes or until tender.

4. Add garlic and next 3 ingredients; cook, stirring constantly, for about 2 minutes. Stir in tomato paste, and cook, stirring constantly, for about 2 minutes.

5. Add chiles, next 2 ingredients, beef, and 1 cup water; bring to a boil. Boil, stirring occasionally, 20 minutes. Add salt to taste. Sprinkle with cornmeal.

6. Cook, stirring constantly, 5 minutes or until thickened. Serve with desired toppings.

Beef Burrito Skillet

Preparation time: 5 minutes

Cooking time: 20 minutes

Gross time: 25 minutes

Serves: 2 to 4 people

Recipe Ingredients:

- 1 lb. ground beef
- ¾ package of taco seasoning mix
- 15.5 oz. can of red kidney beans, drained and rinsed
- 1 cup of your favorite salsa
- 1 cup of water
- 4 6" flour tortillas, cut into 1" pieces
- 1 ½ cup of shredded Colby Jack, or cheddar cheese
- 2 tbsp. of sour cream, or more if needed
- Sliced green onions, for garnish

Optional Garnishes:

- Avocado
- Tomato
- Olives
- Guacamole
- Pico de Gallo

Cooking Instructions:

1. Light and prepare charcoal in your grill. Place a Deep Dish Sizzle Skillet on the grill.

2. Add ground beef to skillet, and cook until browned through, for about 8 to 10 minutes. To the skillet, add taco seasoning, water, salsa, and beans.

3. Stir ingredients to combine and distribute spices evenly. Bring to a simmer; cook for about 5 minutes.

4. Add tortilla pieces, and stir to combine. Top with cheese, and cover grill. When cheese has melted remove from heat.

5. Top with sour cream, green onions, and any other garnish you like. Portion individual servings, or let everyone grab a fork and eat right from the skillet!

Garlic Beef Noodle

Preparation time: 5 minutes

Cooking time: 10 minutes

Gross time 15 minutes

Serves: 2 to 4 people

Recipe Ingredients:

- 2 tablespoon of olive oil
- 1 lb. skirt steak, cut into thin strips
- 4 cloves of garlic, minced
- 1 teaspoon fresh ginger, minced
- ¼ cup of soy sauce
- 2 tablespoons of brown sugar
- 1 teaspoon of sesame oil
- 8 ounces of noodles, (udon, lo mein, linguine etc)
- 2 tablespoons of sliced green onions
- 2 teaspoons of sesame seeds

Cooking Instructions:

1. Cook noodles and in a small bowl mix together brown sugar, soy sauce, and sesame oil. Stir until well combined.

2. Set aside Heat oil over high heat in a large skillet. Once hot, add beef strips. Cook for 2-3 minutes, until beef is browned.

3. Add garlic and ginger to the pan, cook for 1 minute until fragrant. Add soy sauce mixture to the pan.

4. Bring to a simmer, and cook for about 3 to5 minutes until sauce slightly thickens. Add cooked noodles to the pan, stir to coat.

5. Sprinkle green onions and sesame seeds over the pan to serve.

Ground Beef Chili Mac and Cheese

Preparation time: 10 minutes

Cooking time: 20 minutes

Gross time: 30 minutes

Serves: 2 to 4 people

Recipe Ingredients:

- 8 ounces (250g) of dry weight elbow or macaroni pasta, cooked to al dente, drained
- 1 tbsp. of olive oil
- 1 large yellow onion, diced
- ½ green pepper (capsicum), seeded and diced
- 4 cloves of garlic, minced
- 1 pound (500g) of lean ground beef
- 1 tbsp. of each ground cumin and red chili powder or Cayenne
- ½ tsp. of smoked paprika
- ½ tsp. of salt
- 7 ounces (200g) of crushed tomatoes
- 7 ounces (210g) of tomato puree
- 1 cup (250 ml) of beef or chicken broth
- 1 tbsp. of tomato paste
- 14 ounces (400g) of red kidney beans, drained
- 7 ounces (200g) of black beans, drained
- 1 cup of shredded Cheddar Cheese (or Monterey Jack)
- 1 cup of shredded mozzarella cheese

Cooking Instructions:

1. Heat oil in large heavy-based pot (or casserole pot) over medium-high heat.

2. Add onions and sauté until transparent, then add the green peppers (or capsicum) and garlic, sautéing for a further minute until the garlic is fragrant.

3. Add beef and cook until browned, breaking up any big chunks with the end of your wooden spoon.

4. Stir in the cumin, chili powder, paprika and salt and mix through until beef is fully coated in the seasonings.

5. Mix in the crushed tomatoes along with the juices, tomato puree, broth, tomato paste and beans.

6. Bring to a boil, then lower heat and allow to simmer while stirring occasionally, until the chili thickens (about 10 minutes).

7. Preheat oven broiler (or grill) on medium heat. Add the cooked pasta and toss well to combine.

8. Top with cheese, transfer to oven and broil for 2 minutes, or until cheese is bubbling and melted.

9. Garnish with sliced jalapeños and chopped cilantro (optional). Serve with sour cream.

Enchilada Taco Casserole

Preparation time: 5 minutes

Cooking time: 25 minutes

Gross time:30 minutes

Servings: 4 to 6 people

Recipe Ingredients:

- 1 package (16 ounces) of shells pasta
- 1 lb. of extra lean ground beef
- ½ cup of yellow onion
- ½ tsp. of minced garlic
- 1 packet of taco seasoning + 1/4 cup water
- 1 cup of corn
- 1 can (14.5 oz.) of petite diced tomatoes with green chilies*
- ½ cup of salsa
- 1 can (10 oz.) of medium red enchilada sauce
- 2 cups of taco blend or cheddar cheese
- Optional toppings: sour cream, scallions, cilantro, cherry tomatoes

Cooking Instructions:

1. Prepare the pasta, cook until al dente, drain, and set aside. Preheat the oven to 350°F.

2. Meanwhile, in a large saucepan, brown the ground beef until completely cooked through (cook on medium heat).

3. Drain any fat and return the meat to the saucepan. Add in the onion and garlic. Stir and cook on medium heat for about 2 to 3 minutes.

4. Add in the taco seasoning and water. Stir until the meat is well coated with the seasoning.

5. Combine the pasta and meat mixture with the corn, (drained) petite diced tomatoes, and salsa.

6. Pour the mixture into a 9 x 13 casserole dish. Cover with 1 (or 2) cans of red enchilada sauce.

7. Cover with foil and bake for about 20 to 25 minutes. Remove from the oven and top with cheese.

8. Return to the oven without the foil and cook for another 8-10 minutes or until the cheese is melted.

9. Top with optional toppings of choice and serve immediately.

Beef Ragu Pasta

Preparation time: 5 minutes

Cooking time: 8 hours

Overall time: 8 hours 5 minutes

Serves: 2 to 4 people

Recipe Ingredients:

- 1.5 lb. of sirloin cap roast
- 1 tablespoon of olive oil
- Salt & pepper to taste
- 1 (28 oz.) can of crushed tomatoes
- 1 cup of beef broth
- 3 cloves of garlic sliced
- 1 medium onion chopped
- 2 medium Carrots chopped
- 1 teaspoon of dried thyme or 5 springs fresh thyme
- 3 dried bay leaves
- 1 lb. of chickpea pasta or pasta of choice

Optional:

- Grated cheese
- Parsley

Cooking Instructions:

1. Rub sirloin cap roast with oil, generously sprinkle with salt and pepper. Transfer into a slow cooker, fat cap side down.

2. Pour crushed tomatoes on top. Add the beef broth, garlic, onion, carrots, thyme, and bay leaves around the roast.

3. Cook covered on low for about 8 to 9 hours or on high for about 5 to 6 hours. Remove the thyme sprig (if using) and bay leaves.

4. Shred the beef using two forks and cook chickpea pasta, transfer to serving bowls. Pour on the Ragu and serve hot with extra vegetables, such as spinach or kale.

5. Alternatively, add the pasta and the sauce into separate meal prep containers and save for later.

Korean Beef Brisket

Preparation time: 10 minutes

Cooking time: 1 hour 30 minutes

Overall time: 1 hour 40 minutes

Serves: 6 to 8 people

Recipe Ingredients:

- 5 lb. of beef brisket, cut into 3 or 4 pieces
- 1 tablespoon of sweet paprika
- ½ teaspoon of red chili flakes
- 2½ teaspoons of kosher salt, plus more to taste
- ½ teaspoon of freshly ground black pepper
- 1 to 3 tablespoons of peanut oil, as needed
- 1 large onion, diced
- 4 garlic cloves, minced
- 1 tablespoon of grated peeled fresh ginger
- 1 cup of water
- ¼ cup of Gochujang (Korean chili paste)
- 2 tablespoons of ketchup
- 2 tablespoons of soy sauce
- 2 teaspoons of Asian fish sauce
- 1 teaspoon of toasted sesame oil
- Garnish with: rice, kimchi, avocado, sesame seeds, lime, physalis, cilantro

Cooking Instructions:

1. Rub the beef pieces with the chili flakes, paprika, salt and pepper on all sides.

2. Set the electric pressure cooker to sauté. Add a tablespoon of the oil, let it heat up for a few seconds.

3. Add the beef and sear until it's browned all over, for about 2 minutes per side, adding more oil as needed.

4. Transfer the beef to a plate and repeat with the remaining pieces. Add the onion, garlic and ginger sauté until golden, for about 3 to 5 minutes.

5. Add the water, Gochujang, ketchup, soy sauce, fish sauce and sesame oil. Scrape the mixture into the pressure cooker if you have used a skillet.

6. Return all meat to the cooker. Cover and cook on high pressure for 90 minutes. Let the pressure release naturally for about 20 minutes.

7. Release the remaining pressure manually. Transfer the beef to a plate or a rimmed cutting board and tent with foil to keep warm.

8. Set the pressure cooker to sauté and simmer the sauce for 15 to 20 minutes or until reduced by half.

9. Use a fat separator to skim off the fat, or let the sauce settle and spoon the fat off the top. Serve the sauce alongside the beef with kimchi and rice.

Beef & Broccoli Stir Fry

Preparation time: 10 minutes

Cooking time: 15 minutes

Gross time: 25 minutes

Serves: 2 to 4 people

Recipe Ingredients:

- 1 lb. of stew beef, round roast or chuck roast
- 3 cups of broccoli florets
- 2 tablespoons of ghee
- 2 tablespoons of minced garlic
- 2 tablespoons of minced ginger
- Green onions for garnish

Marinade

- 1 tablespoon of olive oil
- 2 teaspoons of tapioca flour
- 2 tablespoons of Coconut Aminos
- Salt & pepper, to taste

Cooking Instructions:

1. In a bowl, mix together the ingredients for the marinade. Add the beef to the bowl and let it sit for about 10 minutes.

2. Bring a large sauté pan to medium heat, place ghee, garlic and ginger in the pan. Cook for 2 to 3 minutes until fragrant.

3. Add the beef and marinade to the pan. Cook 5 to 7 minutes until desired tenderness.

4. The marinade will thicken in the pan as it cooks. Add the broccoli to the pan, cooking another 7 minutes until broccoli is tender.

5. Serve immediately garnished with green onions.

PASTA RECIPES

Chicken Sausage Pasta

Preparation time: 5 minutes

Cooking time: 10 minutes

Overall time: 15 minutes

Recipe Ingredients:

- 1 box of Banza pasta (or other pasta of choice)
- 2 cups of Rao's Homemade pasta sauce
- 1 tbsp. of olive oil
- 1 big bag of frozen mixed vegetables
- 4 fully-cooked chicken sausage links, sliced

Cooking Instructions:

1. Cook pasta until al dente. Meanwhile, add olive oil to a skillet with vegetables and chicken sausage.

2. Cook until vegetables are al dente. Divide pasta and vegetable mixture amongst 4 to 5 glass meal prep containers.

3. Top each with ½ cup of pasta sauce. Cover and refrigerate until ready to eat. Microwave 1-2 minutes and enjoy!

Pesto Chicken Tortellini and Veggies

Preparation time: 20 minutes

Cooking time 20 minutes

Overall time: 40 minutes

Serves: 2 to 4 people

Recipe Ingredients:

- 2 tbsp. of olive oil
- 1 pound of chicken thighs boneless and skinless, sliced into strips
- Salt
- ½ cup of sun-dried tomatoes drained of oil, chopped
- 1 pound of asparagus ends trimmed, cut in half
- ¼ cup of basil pesto or use more
- 1 cup of cherry tomatoes yellow and red, halved
- 1 cup of tortellini uncooked

Cooking Instructions:

1. In a large skillet heat 2 tablespoons olive oil on medium heat.

2. Add sliced chicken thighs (seasoned with salt), ¼ cup of chopped sun-dried tomatoes.

3. Cook everything on medium heat for about 5 to 10 minutes, turning chicken slices over a couple of times, until the chicken is completely cooked through.

4. Remove the chicken and the sun-dried from the skillet, leaving the oil in. Add asparagus (ends trimmed).

5. Season generously with salt, and ¼ cup of sun-dried tomatoes to the same skillet.

6. Cook on medium heat for about 5 to 10 minutes until the asparagus is cooked through, remove the asparagus to a serving plate.

7. Cook tortellini and drain. Add cooked chicken back to the skillet. Add basil pesto.

8. Stir to coat and cook on low-medium heat until the chicken is reheated, 1 or 2 minutes. Remove from heat.

9. Add cooked tortellini and halved cherry tomatoes to the skillet with the chicken. Stir to combine. Add more pesto if desired. Season with more salt if needed.

10. Add chicken, cherry tomatoes and tortellini to the serving plate with asparagus.

White Beans and Pasta with Rosemary Pesto

Preparation time: 5 minutes

Cooking time: 25 minutes

Overall time: 30 minutes

Serves: 2 to 4 people

Recipe Ingredients:

- 1 small yellow onion, peeled and roughly chopped
- 2 cloves of garlic, peeled
- 1 tbsp. of extra virgin olive oil
- 1/8 tsp. of red pepper flakes
- 6 oz. of orecchiette pasta
- ¼ cup of tomato paste
- 1 (14 oz.) can of cannellini white beans, drained and rinsed
- 1 tbsp. of salted butter
- ½ cup of rosemary arugula pesto
- Crusty bread and fresh arugula for serving (optional)

Cooking Instructions:

1. Set a large pot of water on the stove and bring to a boil. Meanwhile, place the onion and garlic in the bowl of a food processor and pulse until pureed.

2. Heat the olive oil in a large pan set over medium heat. Add the onion-garlic puree along with the red pepper flakes.

3. Cook, stirring frequently, until the onions have softened and lost their bite, for about 8 to 10 minutes.

4. Meanwhile, add the pasta to the boiling water and cook 1 or 2-minute shy of al dente.

5. When the pasta is nearly done cooking, add the tomato paste and beans to the onion-garlic mixture. Strain the pasta, reserving one cup of cooking water.

6. Add half of the reserved cooking water to the tomato-onion mixture and cook for about 2 to 3 minutes, until well-combined and slightly reduced.

7. Add the butter and drained almost-al dente pasta to the pan, toss well. Add enough of the remaining cup pasta cooking water to mostly submerge the pasta.

8. Cook until the pasta is tender and the sauce is very thick, another 2 to 3 minutes. Stir half of the pesto into the pasta; taste and add salt as desired.

9. Serve hot, with crusty bread and fresh arugula (optional). Garnish with the remaining pesto.

Lemon Ricotta Asparagus Ravioli

Preparation time: 30 minutes

Cooking time 15 minutes

Gross time: 45 minutes

Serves: 4 to 6 people

Recipe Ingredients:

- 1 bunch asparagus, ends trimmed
- 1 cup of fresh basil
- 1 cup of whole milk ricotta cheese
- ½ cup of grated parmesan cheese
- ¼ cup of roasted pistachios, shelloed
- Juice + zest of 2 lemons
- Kosher salt + pepper
- 40 to 50 circle or square wonton wrappers

White Wine Butter Sauce:

- 4 tbsp. of salted butter
- 2 tbsp. of chopped chives
- 1 tbsp. of chopped fresh thyme
- ½ cup of white wine or chicken broth
- 1 cup of low sodium chicken broth
- Pinch of crushed red pepper

Cooking Instructions:

1. Bring a large pot of salted water to a boil. Add the asparagus and blanch until just tender, for about 1 to 2 minutes. Drain and rinse under cold water.

2. In a food processor, combine ¾ of the asparagus, the basil, ricotta, parmesan, pistachios, lemon zest and juice, and a pinch each of salt and pepper.

3. Pulse until combined and smooth. Lay out about 6 wrappers. Spoon 1 tablespoon of filling into the center of each wrapper. Brush the edges with water.

4. Lay a second wrapper on top of each ravioli. Press down the edges to seal, pressing out all the air. Crimp the edges with a fork.

5. Alternately you can create triangles with the square wrappers if desired. Be sure to keep the ravioli's covered as you work to prevent them from drying out.

6. To make the butter sauce. In a large skillet, melt the butter over medium heat. Add the chives and thyme and cook for about 30 seconds to a minute or until fragrant.

7. Pour in the wine and chicken broth and bring to a boil. Season with salt and pepper and a pinch of crushed red pepper.

8. Cook for about 5 minutes or until the sauce has reduced slightly. Meanwhile, bring a large pot of salted water to a boil.

9. Boil the ravioli in batches for 1 to 2 minutes or until they float. Drain. Divide the ravioli among bowls and ladle the sauce over the ravioli.

10. Top with the remaining asparagus.

Chicken Mushroom Fettuccine

Preparation time: 25 minutes

Cooking time: 15 minutes

Gross time: 40 minutes

Serves: 2 to 4 people

Recipe Ingredients:

- 2 tsp. of vegetable or canola oil
- 8 oz. of boneless, skinless chicken breasts
- 1 cup of fresh sliced mushrooms
- 2 medium garlic cloves, minced
- 2 tsp. of all purpose flour
- 1 cup of chicken broth
- ½ cup of evaporated milk
- 4 tbsp. of whipped cream cheese
- 1 ½ cups of freshly grated Parmesan cheese
- Freshly ground black pepper, to taste
- 2 cups of hot cooked fettuccine
- Chopped fresh parsley, for garnish (optional)

Cooking Instructions:

1. Heat the oil in a large skillet. Add the chicken and cook for about 3 minutes on each side, or until tender and cooked through.

2. Remove the chicken from the pan, let it rest for a couple of minutes, and then slice it into small strips and set aside.

3. Add the mushrooms and garlic to the skillet; cook for 1 minute, stirring. Sprinkle with flour, stirring quickly.

4. Stir in the broth and milk. Reduce heat and simmer for about 3 minutes, until the mixture thickens- stirring occasionally.

5. Stir in the cheeses and pepper. Return the chicken to the skillet; cook, stirring for about 2 minutes, until the chicken warms up.

6. Arrange the fettuccine on four plates. Top with chicken and sauce. Garnish with parsley.

7. Serve and enjoy!

Mushroom Penne with Walnut Pesto

Preparation time: 10 minutes

Cooking time: 30 minutes

Overall time: 40 minutes

Serves: 4 to 6 people

Recipe Ingredients:

For the Pasta:

- 8 oz. of penne pasta
- 4 tbsp. of Land O Lakes butter
- 16 oz. of fresh sliced mushrooms
- ¼ cup of grated or shaved Parmesan cheese
- Salt, pepper, and fresh parsley for topping

For the Walnut Pesto:

- 1 cup of walnuts
- 1 ½ cups of packed greens
- ½ to ¾ cup of shredded Parmesan cheese
- ¼ cup of olive oil
- 1 clove of garlic
- Juice of 1 lemon
- Salt and pepper to taste

Cooking Instructions:

1. Cook the penne pasta according to package directions. Drain and set aside.

2. Toast the walnuts in a small sauté pan over low heat with no butter or oil, stir and shake the pan until the walnuts are fragrant and toasty for about 5 minutes.

3. In a food processor, combine all the ingredients for the walnut pesto and pulse until mostly smooth. Heat the butter over medium heat in a wide skillet.

4. Add the mushrooms and Sauté for about 8 to 10 minutes, until the mushrooms are a deep golden brown.

5. Add the penne pasta to the pan and stir to combine, adding Parmesan, salt, pepper, and fresh parsley or other herbs to taste.

6. Divide the pasta between 4 to 6 bowls and top with a generous spoonful of the walnut pesto OR stir the walnut pesto directly into the pasta.

Easy Mushroom Linguine

Preparation time: 10 minutes

Cooking time: 20 minutes

Overall time: 30 minutes

Serves: 1 to 3 people

Recipe Ingredients:

- 160g (5.5 ounces) of linguine
- 25g (2 tablespoons) of butter
- 250g (9 ounces) of chestnut mushrooms sliced
- 4 cloves of garlic peeled and crushed
- 4 sprigs of fresh thyme leaves only
- Pinch chilli flakes
- Juice of 1/2 lemon
- 40g (1.5 ounces) of parmesan cheese (or vegetarian alternative) grated
- Handful fresh parsley finely chopped
- Salt and pepper

Cooking Instructions:

1. Cook the linguine, meanwhile, heat the butter in a frying pan. Add the mushrooms until soft and golden and any liquid has almost all evaporated.

2. Add the garlic, thyme leaves and chilli flakes and cook for a couple more minutes. Season well. Drain the linguine, reserving a cupful of the cooking water.

3. Add the linguine to the mushrooms along with the lemon juice, parmesan and parsley.

4. Toss everything together and add enough of the reserved cooking water to form a light sauce. Season to taste and serve.

Pasta Salad with Garlic Marinated Tomatoes

Preparation time: 10 minutes

Recipe Ingredients:

- 5 garlic cloves thinly sliced
- ½ cup of extra-virgin olive oil
- 2 lb. of cherry tomatoes sliced in half
- 1 cup of fresh basil leaves torn or thinly sliced
- 4 tbsp. of capers
- 1 tbsp. of lemon juice
- 2 tsp. of finely grated lemon zest plus more for sprinkling
- ¼ tsp. of crushed red-pepper flakes
- 1 tsp. of kosher salt
- 1 tsp. of freshly ground pepper
- 1 lb. of pasta cooked al dente
- 8 oz. of mozzarella bocconcini balls sliced in half

Cooking Instructions:

1. In a small saucepan, cook garlic in oil over medium heat until golden, about 10 minutes, let it cool.

2. Combine the tomatoes, ½ cup of basil, capers, lemon zest, red-pepper flakes, and kosher salt in a large mixing bowl.

3. Pour the garlic oil & chips over tomato mixture, marinate for about 30 minutes, tossing occasionally.

4. Cook the pasta, drain, and add to the bowl with the tomato mixture, bocconcini balls and lemon juice and toss gently.

5. Top with remaining ½ cup of basil and additional lemon zest and salt and pepper to taste. Serve warm or at room temperature.

Butternut Squash Goat Cheese Pasta

Preparation time: 15 minutes

Cooking time: 15 minutes

Overall time 30 minutes

Serves: 4 to 6 people

Recipe Ingredients:

- 1 tsp. of medium butternut squash peeled + left whole (don' cut in half)
- 3 tbsp. of olive oil
- Kosher salt + pepper
- ½ lb. of angel hair pasta
- 1 ½ cups day old sourdough bread finely torn
- 1 tbsp. of fresh chopped oregano
- Salt + pepper toast
- 8 tbsp. of butter
- ½ cup fresh oregano leaves
- 2 oz. of prosciutto finely diced (omit if vegetarian)
- 1/3 cup of grated parmesan cheese
- 4 to 6 oz. of goat cheese crumbled or thinly sliced

Cooking Instructions:

1. Preheat the oven to 425°F. Using a spiralizer, spiral the squash into spaghetti size noodles.

2. Alternately, you can cube the squash as well. Place the butternut noodles on a baking sheet and toss with 1 tablespoon olive oil, salt + pepper.

3. Place in the oven and roast for 5-10 minutes or until the noodles are tender, but not mushy. Remove from the oven. Bring a large pot of salted water to a boil.

4. Boil the pasta until al dente. Reserve 1 cup of pasta cooking before draining. Drain.

5. Meanwhile, heat a large skillet over medium heat and add 2 tablespoons olive oil.

6. Once hot, add the bread crumbs, oregano, salt + pepper and cook, stirring for about 4 to 5 minutes or until toasted and golden.

7. Remove the bread crumbs from the pan to a plate. Place the butter, remaining ½ cup oregano leaves and prosciutto in the skillet.

8. Cook over medium heat until the butter is browned and the prosciutto crisp. Remove from the heat.

9. Add in the butternut squash noodles, half the angel hair pasta and parmesan and toss to coat.

10. If desired add the remaining angel hair pasta and a little of the reserved pasta cooking water to thin the sauce.

11. Divide the pasta among bowls and top with breadcrumbs and goat cheese.

White Beans and Pasta with Rosemary Pesto

Preparation time: 5 minutes

Cooking time: 25 minutes

Overall time: 30 minutes

Serves: 3 to 5 people

Recipe Ingredients:

- 1 small yellow onion, peeled and roughly chopped
- 2 cloves of garlic, peeled
- 1 tbsp. of extra virgin olive oil
- 1/8 tsp. of red pepper flakes
- 6 oz. of orecchiette pasta
- ¼ cup of tomato paste
- 1 (14 oz.) can of cannellini white beans, drained and rinsed
- 1 tbsp. of salted butter
- ½ cup of rosemary arugula pesto
- Crusty bread and fresh arugula for serving (optional)

Cooking Instructions:

1. Set a large pot of water on the stove and bring to a boil. Meanwhile, place the onion and garlic in the bowl of a food processor and pulse until pureed.

2. Heat the olive oil in a large pan set over medium heat. Add the onion-garlic puree along with the red pepper flakes.

3. Cook, stirring frequently, until the onions have softened and lost their bite; for about 8 to 10 minutes.

4. Meanwhile, add the pasta to the boiling water and cook 1 or 2 minutes shy of al dente.

5. When the pasta is nearly done cooking, add the tomato paste and beans to the onion-garlic mixture.

6. Strain the pasta, reserving one cup of cooking water. Add half of the reserved cooking water to the tomato-onion mixture.

7. Cook for about 2 to 3 minutes, until well-combined and slightly reduced. Add the butter and drained almost-al dente pasta to the pan and toss well.

8. Add enough of the remaining half cup pasta cooking water to mostly submerge the pasta.

9. Cook until the pasta is tender and the sauce is very thick, another 2 to 3 minutes. Stir half of the pesto into the pasta; taste and add salt as desired.

10. Serve hot, with crusty bread and fresh arugula (optional). Garnish with the remaining pesto.

Roasted Cauliflower and Mushroom Carbonara

Preparation time: 10 minutes

Cooking time: 40 minutes

Gross time:50 minutes

Serves: 2 to 4 people

Recipe Ingredients:

- 1 small head cauliflower, cut into florets
- 8 oz. of mushrooms, quartered
- 1 tbsp. of olive oil
- Salt and pepper to taste
- 8 oz. of fettuccine
- 4 oz. of pancetta, diced
- 1 clove of garlic, chopped
- 2 eggs
- ½ cup (2 oz.) of parmigiana reggiano (parmesan), grated
- Plenty of fresh cracked black pepper
- Salt to taste
- 1 tbsp. of parsley, chopped

Cooking Instructions:

1. Toss the cauliflower and mushrooms in the oil, salt and pepper, place on a baking sheet in a single layer.

2. Roast in a preheated 400°F oven until they start to caramelize, for about 20 to 30 minutes, mixing half way through.

3. Start cooking the pasta as directed on the package. Cook the pancetta in a pan, pour off all but a tablespoon of the grease from the pan.

4. Add the garlic, cook for about 30 second and turn off the heat. Mix the egg, cheese, pepper and salt and parsley in a bowl. Drain the cooked pasta reserving some of the water.

5. Mix the pasta, egg mixture, cauliflower and mushrooms into the pan with the pancetta, adding reserved pasta water as needed.

Skinny Cajun Shrimp Alfredo Pasta

Preparation time: 10 minutes

Cooking time: 15 minutes

Overall time 25 minutes

Serves: 2 to 4 people

Recipe Ingredients:

- 8 ounces (225g) of pasta
- 1 lb. shrimp (shelled)
- 2 tsp. of olive oil
- 3 tsp. of Cajun seasoning
- 2 tbsp. of unsalted butter
- 2 cloves of garlic, minced
- 2 tbsp. of all-purpose flour
- 1 ¾ cup of milk (I used 2%)
- ½ tsp. of dried thyme
- ½ tsp. of dried oregano
- ¼ tsp. of salt
- ¼ tsp. of pepper
- ¼ cup of shredded parmesan cheese

Cooking Instructions:

1. Cook the pasta according to the package directions in a large pot of boiling water and drain.

2. Meanwhile, heat a non-stick skillet over medium heat. Toss the shrimp with the olive oil and the Cajun seasoning.

3. Add the shrimp to the skillet and cook for about 4 minutes, flipping once, until they are completely pink. Set aside and keep warm.

4. In a medium saucepan, over medium heat, melt the butter. Add the garlic and cook, stirring for about 30 seconds, until fragrant.

5. Whisk in the flour, and cook, whisking constantly, until it is lightly browned, about 1 minute.

6. Slowly whisk in the milk, stirring until it is incorporated and smooth. Add the thyme, oregano, salt, pepper and parmesan.

7. Whisk continuously for about 3 to 4 minutes until the sauce has thickened slightly. Reduce the heat to a low simmer until the pasta is ready.

8. Toss together the pasta and alfredo sauce and serve with the Cajun shrimp on top. Garnish with parsley and additional parmesan if desired.

Cherry Tomato, Basil, Spinach and Parmesan Pasta

Preparation time: 20 minutes

Cooking time: 15 minutes

Overall time: 35 minutes

Serves: 2 to 4 people

Recipe Ingredients:

- 4 oz. of dried spaghetti
- 3 cups of cherry tomatoes
- 2 cups of baby spinach roughly chopped
- 1 bunch basil leaves about 10 to 12 leaves; roughly chopped
- 4 garlic cloves very thinly sliced
- 1 tsp. of dried oregano
- ½ tsp. of sea salt or to taste
- ½ tsp. of black pepper or to taste
- 1/4 cup of grated Parmesan cheese plus more for garnish
- ¼ tsp. of red pepper flakes optional
- 1 red chili pepper deseeded and finely chopped (optional)
- Extra virgin olive oil for frying

Cooking Instructions:

1. Bring a large pot of lightly salted water to a boil. Cook pasta until al dente. Drain and reserve ¾ cups of pasta water.

2. While the pasta is cooking, heat the olive oil in a large frying pan over medium heat.

3. Add the garlic, and gently sauté for about a minute or two, until the garlic is just beginning to color. Add the tomatoes, oregano, salt and black pepper.

4. Cook tomatoes for about 3 to 4 minutes until juices start to burst. Add the chopped chili pepper and cook for another minute or two until slightly softened.

5. Add the cooked pasta and reserved pasta water little by little until pasta is well coated. and consistency is reached.

6. Allow to simmer for about a minute then add the red chili pepper flakes, chopped spinach, basil and Parmesan cheese.

7. Turn heat to low and gently toss to coat evenly. Add more pasta water if needed. Remove from heat.

8. Season more to taste if desired and serve with extra grated Parmesan cheese.

9. Serve and enjoy!

Butternut Squash Goat Cheese Pasta

Preparation time: 15 minutes

Cooking time: 15 minutes

Overall time: 30 minutes

Serves: 4 to 6 people

Recipe Ingredients:

- 1 teaspoon of medium butternut squash peeled
- 3 tbsp. of olive oil
- Kosher salt + pepper
- ½ pound angel hair pasta
- 1 ½ cups of day old sourdough bread finely torn
- 1 tbsp. of fresh chopped oregano
- Salt + pepper toast
- 8 tbsp. of butter
- ½ cup of fresh oregano leaves
- 2 oz. of prosciutto finely diced (omit if vegetarian)
- 1/3 cup of grated parmesan cheese
- 4 to 6 oz. of goat cheese crumbled or thinly sliced

Cooking Instructions:

1. Preheat the oven to 425°F. Using a spiralizer, spiral the squash into spaghetti size noodles.

2. Place the butternut noodles on a baking sheet and toss with 1 tablespoon olive oil, salt + pepper.

3. Place in the oven and roast for about 5 to 10 minutes or until the noodles are tender, but not mushy. Remove from the oven.

4. Bring a large pot of salted water to a boil. Boil the pasta until al dente. Reserve 1 cup of pasta cooking before draining. Drain.

5. Meanwhile, heat a large skillet over medium heat and add 2 tablespoons olive oil. Once hot, add the bread crumbs, oregano, salt + pepper,

6. Cook, stirring for about 4 to 5 minutes or until toasted and golden. Remove the bread crumbs from the pan to a plate.

7. Place the butter, remaining 1/2 cup oregano leaves and prosciutto in the skillet and cook over medium heat until the butter is browned and the prosciutto crisp.

8. Remove from the heat. Add in the butternut squash noodles, half the angel hair pasta and parmesan and toss to coat.

9. If desired add the remaining angel hair pasta and a little of the reserved pasta cooking water to thin the sauce.

10. Divide the pasta among bowls and top with breadcrumbs and goat cheese. EAT!

Ratatouille Spaghetti

Preparation time: 10 minutes

Cooking time: 12 minutes

Overall time: 22 minutes

Serves: 2 to 4 people

Recipe Ingredients:

- 1 tablespoon of olive oil
- ½ white onion, diced
- 3 cloves of garlic, minced
- 1 medium courgette, zucchini, diced
- 1/2 aborigine, eggplant, diced
- 1 red pepper, diced
- 400g tin of chopped tomatoes
- 480ml of boiled water
- 1 teaspoon of balsamic vinegar
- 150g of dried gluten-free spaghetti,
- 1 tablespoon of chopped basil
- Salt and pepper, to taste
- 2 tablespoons of nutritional yeast flakes,

Cooking Instructions:

1. Heat the olive oil in a frying pan. Add the onions, garlic, courgette, aubergine and peppers.

2. Cook for a few minutes on a high heat until lightly browned. Add the chopped tomatoes, water, vinegar and spaghetti.

3. Bring to a boil then simmer for 10 minutes until the pasta is cooked and the sauce has thickened.

4. Stir in the chopped basil and add salt and pepper, to taste. Add the nutritional yeast, if using. Serve and enjoy!

Pasta Salad with Garlic Marinated Tomatoes

Preparation time: 5 minutes

Cooking time: 25 minutes

Gross time: 30 minutes

Serves: 2 to 4 people

Recipe Ingredients:

- 5 garlic cloves thinly sliced
- ½ cup of extra-virgin olive oil
- 2 lb. of cherry tomatoes sliced in half
- 1 cup of fresh basil leaves torn or thinly sliced
- 4 tbsp. of capers
- 1 tbsp. of lemon juice
- 2 tsp. of finely grated lemon zest plus more for sprinkling
- ¼ tsp. of crushed red-pepper flakes
- 1 tsp. of kosher salt
- 1 tsp. of freshly ground pepper
- 1 lb. of pasta cooked al dente
- 8 oz. of mozzarella bocconcini balls sliced in half

Cooking Instructions:

1. In a small saucepan, cook garlic in oil over medium heat until golden, for about 10 minutes. Let cool.

2. Combine the tomatoes, ½ cup basil, capers, lemon zest, red-pepper flakes, and kosher salt in a large mixing bowl.

3. Pour the garlic oil & chips over tomato mixture, marinate for about 30 minutes, tossing occasionally.

4. Cook the pasta, drain, and add to the bowl with the tomato mixture, bocconcini balls and lemon juice and toss gently.

5. Top with remaining ½ cup basil and additional lemon zest and salt and pepper to taste. Serve warm or at room temperature.

Avocado Sauce Pasta

Preparation time: 5 minutes

Cooking time: 10 minutes

Overall time: 15 minutes

Serves: 1 to 3 people

Recipe Ingredients:

- 2 cups of uncooked dry pasta any type
- 1 ripe avocado halved, seeded and peeled
- ¼ cup of olive oil
- ¼ cup of grated parmesan or romano cheese
- ¼ cup of fresh basil leaves or/and cilantro or parsley
- 2 cloves of garlic
- 2 tbsp. of lemon or lime juice
- Salt and freshly ground black pepper to taste

Cooking Instructions:

1. Cook your pasta and drain well.

2. While the pasta is cooking, place the avocado, olive oil, parmesan cheese, garlic, cilantro, and lime juice in a blender or food processor and blend well.

3. You can leave it chunky or process it until it's creamy. Toss the pasta with the avocado sauce.

4. Season with salt and pepper to taste and top with parmesan or romano cheese, if desired. Enjoy!

FISH AND SEAFOOD RECIPES

Teriyaki Tofu

Preparation time: 5 minutes

Ingredients:

Sauce:

- 1 tbsp. of corn starch,
- 1 tbsp. of cold water,
- 1 tbsp. of brown sugar,
- ½ cup of soy sauce,
- ¼ cup apple cider vinegar,
- 1 tsp. of fresh grated ginger,
- 1 garlic clove, minced,
- black pepper for seasoning,
- Juice of half a lime.

Tofu and The Rest:

- 200g of block of tofu,
- Quinoa or Rice of your choice,
- Kale

Cooking Instructions:

1. Mix the water and corn starch together to form a slurry. Add this into a medium sized saucepan along with all the other ingredients.

2. Heat over a medium heat and stir constantly with a whisk to avoid any sauce sticking to the bottom.

3. Once the sauce begins to bubble it will thicken very quickly. Once the sauce coats the back of a spoon it is ready.

4. Transfer it immediately to another container to stop the cooking process. Cut the tofu into slices around ¼ inch thick and lay on a tray.

5. Cover with 3 to 4 tablespoons of teriyaki sauce and leave to marinade for a minimum of 30 minutes, or up to overnight.

6. Cook the tofu on a hot griddle pan until hot all the way through. Serve with quinoa and sautéed kale, and top with the cashews, spring onions and cress.

Wild Rice Power

Preparation time: 5 minutes

Cooking time: 30 minutes

Overall time: 35 minutes

Serves: 1 to 3 people

Recipe Ingredients:

- ½ cup of wild rice, uncooked
- 3 large carrots, peeled and chopped
- 1 large red bell pepper
- ½ large avocado
- ¼ cup of hummus

Cooking Instructions:

1. Cook wild rice and place chopped carrots and whole pepper on a foil lined baking sheet.

2. Drizzle with olive oil and roast and 425°F for about 20 to 25 min, stirring the carrots occasionally.

3. Remove vegetables, peel skin from pepper, remove seeds and slice into strips. Divide rice and veggies between two bowls.

4. Top each with avocado slices and hummus. Serve warm or cold!

Mayo Scrambled Eggs & Smoked Salmon

Preparation time: 5 minutes

Cooking time: 10 minutes

Overall time: 15 minutes

Serves: 1 to 3 people

Recipe Ingredients:

- 2 sliced smoked salmon
- 2 large eggs
- ½ tablespoon of extra virgin olive oil
- 1 tablespoon of mayo, divided
- ½ cup of baby spinach
- 4 grape tomatoes, sliced in half
- Fresh dill for garnish
- Salt & pepper to taste

Cooking Instructions:

1. Heat extra virgin olive oil in a small skillet over medium heat. Add tomatoes and spinach. Cook until spinach is slightly wilted.

2. Next stir the egg into the veggies with 1 tablespoon of the mayo and salt and pepper. Once the eggs are almost done cooking, add the salmon.

3. Turn off the heat. Transfer to a plate and garnish with fresh dill.

Power Burrito from Chef Andrew Gruel

Preparation time: 5 minutes

Cooking time: 18 minutes

Overall time: 23 minutes

Serves: 2 to 4 people

Recipe Ingredients:

- 6 to 8 ounces of Regal Springs Tilapia Filet
- 2 Each 13-inch tortilla shell
- 1 tbsp. of extra virgin olive oil
- 1 Lemon – juice and zest
- 1 tbsp. of fresh thyme

For The Filling:

- 1 ripe avocado diced
- 1 cup of cooked quinoa
- 1 cup of raw spinach
- 2 tbsp. of sliced carrot
- 2 tbsp. of crushed toasted almond
- 6 slices of tomato
- **For The Dressing:**
- 1 tbsp. of plain yogurt
- 1 tsp. of flaxseed
- 1 tsp. of cider vinegar
- 1 tsp. of chopped cilantro
- 1 tsp. of Red Sauce
- Garnish
- Radish
- Cilantro
- Thinly Sliced Red Onion

Cooking Instructions:

1. Rub Tilapia filet with olive oil, salt, pepper, and top with fresh thyme. Place in oven and bake for about 18 minutes until flakey.

2. While the fish is cooking, combine the filling ingredients in a single bowl. Whisk together the dressing and toss lightly with filling ingredients.

3. Lay the burrito shells on a large countertop and top with filling ingredients. Top with hot fish when out of oven. Drizzle with more sauce if needed.

4. Roll burritos and grill/sear on the outside until warm and toasted. Slice in the center and garnish.

Broccoli and Bow Ties

Preparation time: 15 minutes

Cooking time: 8 minutes

Overall time: 23 minutes

Serves: 6 to 8 people

Recipe Ingredients:

- Kosher salt
- 8 cups of broccoli florets (4 heads)
- ½ lb. of farfalle (bow tie) pasta
- 2 tbsp. of unsalted butter
- 2 tbsp. of olive oil
- 1 tsp. of minced garlic
- 1 lemon, zested
- ½ tsp. of freshly ground black pepper
- 1 tbsp. of freshly squeezed lemon juice
- ¼ cup toasted pignoli (pine) nuts
- Freshly grated Parmesan, optional

Cooking Instructions:

1. Cook the broccoli for 3 minutes in a large pot of boiling salted water. Remove the broccoli from the water with a slotted spoon or sieve.

2. Place in a large bowl and set aside. In the same water, cook the bow-tie pasta for about 12 minutes. Drain well and add to the broccoli.

3. Meanwhile, in a small Sauté pan, heat the butter and oil and cook the garlic and lemon zest over medium-low heat for 1 minute.

4. Off the heat, add 2 teaspoons of salt, the pepper, and lemon juice and pour this over the broccoli and pasta.

5. Toss well. Season to taste, sprinkle with the pignolis and cheese, if using, and serve.

6. To toast pignolis, place them in a dry Sauté pan over medium-low heat and cook, tossing often, for about 5 minutes, until light brown.

Baked Lemon Butter Tilapia

Preparation time: 10 minutes

Cooking time: 10 minutes

Overall time: 20 minutes

Serves: 2 to 4 people

Recipe Ingredients:

- ¼ cup of unsalted butter, melted
- 3 cloves of garlic, minced
- 2 tbsp. of freshly squeezed lemon juice, or more, to taste
- Zest of 1 lemon
- 4 (6 oz.) of tilapia fillets
- Kosher salt and freshly ground black pepper, to taste
- 2 tbsp. of chopped fresh parsley leaves

Cooking Instructions:

1. Preheat oven to 425°F. Lightly oil a 9×13 baking dish or coat with nonstick spray.

2. In a small bowl, whisk together butter, garlic, lemon juice and lemon zest; set aside.

3. Season tilapia with salt and pepper, to taste and place onto the prepared baking dish. Drizzle with butter mixture.

4. Place into oven and bake until fish flakes easily with a fork, for about 10 to 12 minutes. Serve immediately, garnished with parsley, if desired.

One Pan Fajita Salmon

Preparation time: 10 minutes

Cooking time: 18 minutes

Overall time: 28 minutes

Serves: 2 to 4 people

Recipe Ingredients:

- 1 lb. of sockeye salmon
- 1 large onion sliced
- 2 large peppers sliced
- 1 ½ tablespoons of olive oil
- Fajita seasoning

Cooking Instructions:

1. Preheat your oven to 375ºF. Place your sockeye salmon and sliced veggies on a baking sheet.

2. Drizzle with olive oil and sprinkle with fajita seasoning. Toss Veggies Bake for about 18 minutes or until cooked as desired.

3. Divide into containers and enjoy within 4 days of cooking

Lemon-Garlic Salmon Foil Packets

Preparation time: 10 minutes

Cooking time: 30 minutes

Overall time: 40 minutes

Serves: 2 to 4 people

Recipe Ingredients:

- 4 (3 to 4 oz.) pieces of wild caught sockeye salmon fillets
- ½ pound of mini potatoes (a mixture of purple, red and gold)
- ½ an onion
- 1 large zucchini
- 2 tablespoons of avocado oil
- Himalayan sea salt
- Cracked black pepper
- 4 lemon slices (halved)

Marinade:

- 2 tablespoons of Cultured ghee
- 2 tablespoons of Coconut aminos
- 1 tablespoon of lemon juice
- 2 finely minced garlic cloves
- 1 tablespoon of finely chopped cilantro leaves
- 2 tablespoons of finely chopped parsley
- ½ teaspoon of Himalayan sea salt

Cooking Instructions:

1. First, preheat oven to 400ºF. Now, cut out 4 (10 to 12 inch) pieces of heavy duty foil and place one piece of salmon in the center of each foil sheet.

2. Now, clean and cut potatoes into quarters, drizzle with avocado oil and cook in a microwave for approx. for about 3 minutes.

3. Now, cube onion and zucchini into about ½ an inch piece; transfer them to the bowl with the potatoes and season with a couple pinches of salt and pepper.

4. Now, whisk all marinade ingredients in a bowl. To put the packets together, divide potato mixture into 4 portions.

5. Add them alongside the salmon in the center of each foil sheet. Then, add an equal portion of the marinade atop each piece of salmon.

6. Finish with lemon slices. Seal the tops and sides of each foil packet and transfer to a large baking sheet.

7. Bake for about 20 to 25 minutes. Then, remove from oven, open packets, turn the oven to broil and return the packets to the oven for about 5 minutes.

8. Let packets rest for a few minutes, and transfer them to a plate. Serve with a fresh salad and enjoy!

Easy Quinoa Fish Taco Bowls

Preparation time: 5 minutes

Cooking time: 10 minutes

Overall time: 15 minutes

Serves: 2 to 4 people

Recipe Ingredients:

- 1 ½ tsp. of paprika
- ¾ tsp. of garlic powder
- ½ tsp. of salt
- ½ tsp. of ground cumin
- ¼ tsp. of ground red pepper
- 4 (6 oz.) of tilapia fillets
- 1 tbsp. of coconut oil, for cooking
- 2 cups of cooked quinoa
- 1 (15 oz.) can of corn, drained
- 1 (15 oz.) can of black beans, drained and rinsed
- ½ cup of shredded cabbage
- 1 avocado, sliced
- 1 lime
- Cilantro, to taste

Cooking Instructions:

1. Combine first 5 seasoning ingredients.

2. Pat the tilapia fillets dry and sprinkle both sides with the seasoning blend. Heat coconut oil in a large skillet.

3. Cook tilapia on both sides until it's no longer translucent, until the flesh starts to flake. Remove and let cool before cutting into 1-inch pieces.

4. To assemble bowls, layer quinoa with tilapia, corn, black beans, shredded cabbage, and ¼ avocado.

5. Garnish with lime and cilantro. Enjoy!

Butter Roasted Split Pea Power

Preparation time: 5 minutes

Cooking time: 15 minutes

Gross time: 20 minutes

Serves: 1 to 3 people

Recipe Ingredients:

- 1 cup of split Peas
- 1 large ripe avocado
- 80g of smoked salmon (2.8 ounces)
- 60g of feta cheese (2 ounces)
- 30g of unsalted butter (1 ounce)
- A handful of fresh flat leaf parsley
- A squeeze of lemon (optional)
- Salt to taste

Cooking Instructions:

1. Soak split peas in cold water overnight in order to reduce the cooking time. Now drain the soaked peas, transfer back into a pot and pour 3 cups of water in.

2. Bring to the boil, reduce the heat and simmer for about 20 minutes. Drain the water. In a frying pan, melt the butter over a medium heat.

3. Throw in drained split peas. Increase the heat and roast for 3 minutes, stirring occasionally. Add roughly chopped parsley.

4. Roast for a further 2 to 3 minutes before turning off the heat. For the toppings: Wash & peel the avocado.

5. Remove the stone and cut into slices/cubes. Slice smoked salmon, crumble/dice feta cheese.

6. Divide all the ingredients in 2 bowl and serve warm or cold!

SALAD AND VEGETABLE RECIPES

Roasted Cauliflower with Tahini-Cilantro Vinaigrette

Preparation time: 15 minutes

Cooking time: 30 minutes

Overall time: 45 minutes

Serves: 4 to 6 people

Recipe Ingredients:

For the Cauliflower:

- 2 heads cauliflower, cut into small florets
- 2 tbsp. of melted coconut oil
- ½ tsp. of sea salt (Pink Himalayan is wonderful)
- Freshly ground black pepper, to taste

For the Tahini-Cilantro Vinaigrette:

- 1/3 cup of chopped fresh cilantro, plus more for garnishing
- ¼ cup of extra-virgin olive oil
- 2 tbsp. of fresh lime juice
- 1 ½ tbsp. of apple cider vinegar
- 1 tbsp. of tahini
- 1 tsp. of agave nectar
- 1 clove of garlic, minced
- ¼ tsp. of sea salt, plus more for garnishing
- Freshly ground black pepper, to taste

Cooking Instructions:

1. Preheat oven to 425°F. Line a large baking sheet with parchment paper and spread the cauliflower florets out over the pan.

2. Drizzle them with the coconut oil and sprinkle with salt and pepper. Toss the florets to coat them in the oil and seasonings.

3. Roast the cauliflower for about 25 to 30 minutes or until you can see hints of golden edges of the florets. Let cool slightly.

4. In a small mixing bowl, whisk together the cilantro, olive oil, lime juice, apple cider vinegar, tahini, agave, garlic, sea salt, and black pepper.

5. Transfer the warm cauliflower to a large bowl, pour the vinaigrette over top, and toss to coat. Serve, garnish, and enjoy.

6. Refrigerate leftovers.

Simple Roasted Carrots

Preparation time: 10 minutes

Cooking time: 20 minutes

Overall time: 30 minutes

Serves: 2 to 4 people

Recipe Ingredients:

- 8 carrots
- 1 tbsp. of olive oil
- ½ tsp. of paprika
- 1/8 tsp. salt
- 1/8 tsp. of pepper

Cooking Instructions:

1. Preheat oven to 425°F. Cut carrots into 1-inch slices on the diagonal and place on a rimmed baking sheet.

2. Whisk together olive oil, paprika, salt and pepper in a small bowl. Pour over carrots and toss to coat.

3. Roast carrots in the oven for about 20 minutes, stirring after 10 minutes, until crisp-tender. Serve.

Simple Lemon Green Beans

Preparation time: 10 minutes

Cooking time: 5 minutes

Overall time: 15 minutes

Serves: 2 to 4 people

Recipe Ingredients:

- 1 lb. of green beans, de-stemmed
- 2 tbsp. of extra-virgin olive oil
- 1 garlic clove, grated or finely minced
- Juice of ½ lemon plus ½ teaspoon zest
- Sea salt and freshly ground black pepper.

Cooking Instructions:

1. Bring a large pot of water to a boil. In a small bowl mix together the olive oil, garlic, lemon juice, zest, salt, and pepper.

2. Boil the beans until tender but still vibrant green and a little bit crunchy, for about 2 to 4 minutes. The timing will depend on their size.

3. Drain the green beans in a colander, and rinse under cold water. Transfer to a kitchen towel and pat dry.

4. Transfer to a serving dish and toss with the dressing. Season to taste and serve.

Healthy Broccoli Salad

Preparation time: 5 minutes

Cooking time: 10 minutes

Overall time: 15 minutes

Serves: 2 to 4 people

Recipe Ingredients:

- 1 head of broccoli cut into bite-size florets
- ½ medium red onion chopped finely
- 1 small apple, cut into small pieces
- ½ cup of dried cranberries
- 1/3 cup of sliced almonds

Dressing:

- ½ cup of Greek yogurt (I used 2%)
- 1 heaping tablespoon mayo
- 1 tbsp. of honey
- ½ tbsp. of cider vinegar
- Salt & pepper to taste

Cooking Instructions:

1. Prep the broccoli, onion, and apple. Add them to a large salad bowl along with the dried cranberries and sliced almonds.

2. Whisk the dressing ingredients together. Pour the dressing over the salad and toss well.

3. Season with extra salt & pepper if needed. Serve immediately or chill first. Can be made a few hours ahead.

Chickpea Salad

Preparation time: 10 minutes

Cooking time: 15 minutes

Overall time 25 minutes

Serves: 2 to 4 people

Recipe Ingredients:

For the salad:

- 2 cups of canned chickpeas drained and rinsed
- 1 avocado peeled, pit removed, and diced
- 1 cup of cherry tomatoes halved
- 1 cup of cucumbers quartered and sliced
- ¼ cup of red onion finely diced
- ½ cup of crumbled feta cheese
- ¼ cup of chives thinly sliced
- Additional chives and feta for garnish optional

For the dressing:

- ¼ cup of olive oil
- 1 tsp. of Dijon mustard
- 2 tbsp. of red wine vinegar
- 1 tbsp. of lemon juice
- ¼ tsp. of garlic powder
- ¼ tsp. of onion powder
- ½ tsp. of dried oregano
- Salt and pepper to taste

Cooking Instructions:

1. Place the chickpeas, avocado, tomatoes, cucumbers, red onion, feta cheese and chives in a large bowl.

2. Combine all of the ingredients in a jar and shake vigorously to combine. Store in the refrigerator for up to one week.

3. Pour the dressing over the vegetables and toss gently to coat. Garnish with additional feta and chives if desired, then serve.

Avocado Ranch Chopped Salad with Roasted Chickpeas

Preparation time: 5 minutes

Cooking time: 40 minutes

Overall time: 45 minutes

Serves: 1 to 3 people

Recipe Ingredients:

- 1 (15 oz.) can chickpeas, rinsed and drained
- 1 tbsp. of olive oil
- 1 tsp. of smoked paprika
- ½ tsp. of garlic powder
- 1/4 tsp. of sea salt
- 1/8 tsp. of ground cumin
- 1/8 tsp. of cayenne
- 1/8 tsp. of onion powder
- 1 (12 oz.) bag of Avocado Ranch Chopped Salad

Cooking Instructions:

1. Preheat the oven to 400°F. Thoroughly dry the rinsed chickpeas by patting them with a dish towel or thick paper towel.

2. Remove and discard any chickpea shells that become loose. Spread chickpeas evenly onto a baking sheet.

3. Add olive oil, smoked paprika, garlic powder, sea salt, ground cumin, cayenne and onion powder.

4. Mix together until the chickpeas are thoroughly coated with the seasonings. Bake in oven for about 40 minutes, checking every 15 minutes to make sure chickpeas are browning evenly.

5. Remove from oven when chickpeas are a light golden brown. Let the roasted chickpeas cool for about 5 minutes.

6. In a large mixing bowl, add the entire contents of the Avocado Ranch Chopped Salad, including the topping packets and the dressing.

7. Add the roasted chickpeas and toss together to mix. Divide into 2 separate salad bowls and enjoy!

Mediterranean Bean Salad

Preparation time: 5 minutes

Cooking time: 10 minutes

Overall time: 15 minutes

Serves: 6 to 8 people

Recipe Ingredients:

- 15 oz. can of cannellini beans, drained and well rinsed
- 15 oz. can of garbanzo beans (chickpeas) drained and well rinsed
- 1 cup of cherry tomato halves
- 2 small Persian cucumbers, halved lengthwise and thinly sliced (do not peel)
- ¼ red onion, thinly sliced
- ½ cup of peppadew peppers, rough chopped
- ½ cup of black olives, halved
- ½ cup of pimento stuffed green olives, halved
- 1 cup of assorted colorful bell peppers, diced
- ½ cup of crumbled feta cheese
- ½ cup of chopped marinated artichokes
- About 10 large basil leaves, shredded

Dressing:

- ¼ cup of extra virgin olive oil
- 4 tablespoons of red wine vinegar, or more to taste
- 1 teaspoon of dried Italian herbs
- 1 garlic clove, minced
- Salt and fresh cracked black pepper to taste

Cooking Instructions:

1. Whisk the dressing ingredients together and taste to adjust any of them.

2. Add more vinegar if you want a tangier flavor. Set aside. Put the beans in a large salad bowl.

3. Add the rest of the ingredients and toss with a generous amount of the dressing. The salad will keep, well covered, for several days in the refrigerator.

Detox Kale Salad

Preparation time: 5 minutes

Cooking time: 10 minutes

Overall time: 15 minutes

Serves: 2 to 4 people

Recipe Ingredients:

For the dressing:

- 1/3 cup of grapeseed oil
- ½ cup of lemon juice, fresh
- 1 tbsp. of fresh ginger, peeled and grated
- 2 tsp. of whole grain mustard
- 2 tsp. of pure maple syrup, optional
- ¼ tsp. of salt, or to taste

For the salad:

- 2 cups of dinosaur kale, tightly packed and thinly sliced
- 2 cups of red cabbage, thinly sliced
- 2 cups of broccoli florets
- 2 large carrots, peeled and grated
- 1 red bell pepper, sliced into matchsticks
- 2 avocados, peeled and diced
- ½ cup of fresh parsley, chopped
- 1 cup of walnuts
- 1 tbsp. of sesame seeds

Cooking Instructions:

1. Whisk together all ingredients for the dressing and set aside until ready to use.

2. Add the kale, cabbage, broccoli, bell pepper, and carrots to a large serving bowl.

3. Pour desired amount of dressing over the salad and toss until everything is coated.

4. Add the parsley, diced avocado, sesame seeds and walnuts and toss again. Serve as an entrée salad or as a side salad to your favorite meal.

Easy Roasted Veggies

Preparation time: 15 minutes

Cooking time: 20 minutes

Overall time: 35 minutes

Recipe Ingredients:

- 1 medium sweet potato — peeled and chopped
- 5 cups of kale — chopped
- 1 head of cauliflower — cut into florets
- 2 cups of green beans — chopped
- 2 tbsp. of olive oil
- 1 tsp. of garlic powder
- 1 tsp. of turmeric
- Salt and black pepper to taste
- 4 boiled eggs — cut into half

Cooking Instructions:

1. Preheat the oven to 425°F degrees. Line a baking sheet with parchment paper.

2. Arrange your vegetables (except green beans) in a single layer on the prepared baking sheet.

3. Toss with olive oil, garlic powder, turmeric, salt and pepper. Roast for about 15 to 20 minutes.

4. Then, remove from the oven, add the green beans, return the baking sheet to the oven and roast for about 10 minutes or until all the veggies are tender.

5. Divide roasted veggies between four 22 or 24 ounces of meal prep containers and add the eggs on top.

6. Store in the fridge for up to 4 days. Enjoy!

Savory Roasted Vegetables

Preparation time: 5 minutes

Cooking time: 30minutes

Overall time: 30minutes

Serves: 2 to 4 people

Recipe Ingredients:

- 1 medium sweet potato
- 3 red potatoes
- 4 fingerling purple potatoes
- 2 carrots
- 1 small head of broccoli

Seasonings:

- 2.5 tablespoon of safflower oil (or olive oil)
- 2 sprigs rosemary
- 1.5 teaspoons of garlic powder
- 1.5 teaspoons of oregano
- Juice from 1 lemon
- Sea salt & pepper to taste

Cooking Instructions:

1. Set oven to 420ºF. Chop up your veggies. Slice carrots in half, cut the potatoes into chunky cubes and remove the stems from the broccoli.

2. Place in a bowl. In a small bowl, mix together the ingredients for the seasonings. Pour the seasonings over the vegetables and mix together well.

3. Spread the contents on a baking sheet. Sprinkle a bit of sea salt & pepper on top, then place in the oven.

4. Bake for about 30 minutes. Serve immediately and Enjoy!

Grilled Garlic and Thyme Radishes

Preparation time: 10 minutes

Cooking time: 8 minutes

Overall time: 18 minutes

Serves: 2 to 4 people

Recipe Ingredients:

- 3 cups of radishes, stems removed and halved lengthwise
- 1 tablespoon of ghee, melted
- 2 garlic cloves, minced
- 2 tablespoons of olive oil
- 2 teaspoons of fresh thyme, minced
- 2 teaspoons fresh parsley, minced
- Sea salt and freshly ground black pepper

Cooking Instructions:

1. Preheat grill to medium heat. Place the cut radishes in a bowl, drizzle with olive oil and season to taste with salt and pepper.

2. Add the thyme, garlic, parsley, and melted ghee. Toss until radishes are well coated. Place the radishes on the grill in a grilling basket.

3. Cook until radishes are soft, adjust seasoning, and sprinkle with more fresh thyme before serving.

Garlic Parmesan Roasted Broccoli

Preparation time: 5 minutes

Cooking time: 10 minutes

Overall time: 15 minutes

Serves: 2 to 4 people

Recipe Ingredients:

- 24 oz. of broccoli florets*
- 3 tbsp. of olive oil
- 4 cloves of garlic, minced
- Kosher salt and freshly ground black pepper, to taste
- ¼ cup of freshly grated Parmesan
- Juice of 1 lemon

Cooking Instructions:

1. Preheat oven to 425°F. Lightly oil a baking sheet or coat with nonstick spray. Place broccoli florets in a single layer onto the prepared baking sheet.

2. Add olive oil and garlic; season with salt and pepper, to taste. Gently toss to combine. Place into oven and bake for about 10 to 12 minutes, or until tender.

3. Serve immediately, sprinkled with Parmesan and lemon juice.

Smoked Paprika Roasted Asparagus

Preparation time: 3 minutes

Cooking time: 12 minutes

Overall time: 15 minutes

Serves: 2 to 4 people

Recipe Ingredients:

- 1 lb. of asparagus
- 2 tsp. of olive oil
- ½ tsp. of smoked paprika
- 1/8 tsp. of salt
- 1/8 tsp. of ground pepper

Cooking Instructions:

1. Preheat the oven to 400°F. Trim the tough ends from the asparagus and place the asparagus on a baking sheet.

2. Toss the asparagus with olive oil, smoked paprika, salt and pepper until coated. Arrange in a single layer on the baking sheet.

3. Roast the asparagus until it is just tender, for about 10 to 15 minutes (depending on the thickness of the asparagus). Serve immediately and Enjoy!

Crock Pot Butternut Squash

Preparation time: 1 minutes

Cooking time: 6 hours

Overall time: 6 hours

Serves: 2 to 4 people

Recipe Ingredients:

- 1 medium butternut squash washed

Cooking Instructions:

1. Place whole squash in a slow cooker.

2. Cook until soft and easily pierced, for about 4 to 5 hours on high or 6 to 8 hours on low.

3. When cool enough to handle, cut in half and scoop out seeds.

GRAINS AND BEANS RECIPE

Chickpea Nuggets

Preparation time: 10 minutes

Cooking time: 20 minutes

Overall time: 30 minutes

Serves: 2 to 4 people

Recipe Ingredients:

- ½ cup of panko or gluten-free breadcrumbs
- ½ cup of rolled oats
- (15 oz.) can of garbanzo beans (do not drain)
- 1 tsp. of kosher salt
- ½ tsp. of garlic powder
- ½ tsp. of onion powder

Cooking Instructions:

1. Arrange a rack in the middle of the oven and heat to 375°F. Place the panko on a rimmed baking sheet and bake until toasted and golden-brown, about 5 minutes.

2. Transfer to a bowl and set aside to cool while preparing the nuggets. Line the baking sheet with parchment paper.

3. Place the oats in a food processor fitted with the blade attachment and process into a fine flour. Transfer to a large bowl and reserve the food processor.

4. Drain the chickpeas over a bowl or measuring cup, then save the chickpeas and ¼ cup of the liquid.

5. Place the chickpeas into the food processor; add the salt, garlic, and onion powder; and pulse until crumbly. Keep mixture in the food processor.

6. Whisk ¼ cup of the chickpea liquid in a small mixing bowl until foamy. Add the foamy chickpea liquid and ½ cup of the oat flour to the food processor.

7. Pulse until the mixture forms a ball. You may have a little oat flour leftover, which you can add to the chickpea mixture 1 tablespoon at a time if the mixture is loose.

8. Divide the chickpea mixture into 12 equal portions and shape each one into a nugget.

9 Coat each nugget completely in the toasted panko and place on the parchment-lined baking sheet.

10 Bake until crispy, for about 15 to 20 minutes. Serve warm with your favorite dipping sauce.

Marinated White Beans

Prep time: 5 minutes

Cooking time: 5 minutes

Gross time: 10 minutes

Serves: 4 to 6 people

Recipe Ingredients:

- 1/3 cup of olive oil
- Finely grated zest of 1 medium lemon
- Juice of 1 medium lemon
- 1 medium shallot, diced (about 1/4 cup)
- 1 clove of garlic, grated or minced
- ½ tsp. of kosher salt, plus more as needed
- Freshly ground black pepper
- 2 (15 oz.) cans of cannellini beans, drained and rinsed
- 1/3 cup of chopped fresh flat-leaf parsley leaves
- ¼ cup of chopped fresh oregano leaves

Cooking Instructions:

1 Place the olive oil, lemon zest and juice, shallot, garlic, salt, and few generous grinds of black pepper in a large bowl and whisk to combine.

2 Add the white beans, parsley, and oregano and toss to combine. Taste and season with more salt and pepper as needed.

3 Cover and refrigerate for at least 20 minutes or overnight. Let come to room temperature before serving.

Swiss Chard with Garbanzo Beans

Preparation time: 5 minutes

Cooking time: 10 minutes

Overall time:

Serves: 4 to 6 people

Recipe Ingredients:

- 2 pounds Swiss chard, preferably rainbow chard
- 2 tablespoons extra-virgin olive oil
- 2 ounces pancetta, cut into 1/4-inch dice (about 1/2 cup)
- 2 tablespoons finely chopped shallot
- Pinch red pepper flakes
- 1 can garbanzo beans, drained and rinsed
- Salt
- Freshly ground black pepper

Cooking Instructions:

1 Wash the chard leaves and stems well in a large sink of cold water. Lift the chard out of the water, leaving the grit at the bottom of the sink.

2 Shake off the excess water, but do not dry the chard. Tear the stems from the leaves and chop the stems crosswise into ½ inch pieces; set aside.

3 Stack the leaves and coarsely chop them. Keep the stems and leaves separate. Heat the oil in a large skillet over medium-high heat.

4 Add the pancetta and cook until crisp and browned, about 3 minutes. Stir in the shallot and red pepper flakes.

5 Cook, stirring often, until the shallot softens, for about 2 minutes. Add the chard stems and beans.

6 Cook, stirring occasionally, until the stems soften, for about 4 minutes. Stir in the leaves a handful at a time until wilted.

7 Cover and cook, stirring occasionally, until the chard is tender, for about 5 minutes. Taste and season with salt and pepper as needed. Serve hot.

Black Bean & Corn Salsa

Preparation time: 5 minutes

Cooking time: 10 minutes

Gross time: 15 minutes

Serves: 3 to 5 people

Recipe Ingredients:

- 1 (15.5 oz.) can of black beans, drained and rinsed
- 1 heaping cup of fresh or thawed frozen corn kernels
- 1 medium plum tomato, seeded and diced
- ½ small red onion, diced
- ½ cup of finely chopped fresh cilantro leaves and tender stems
- 1 canned chipotle chile in adobo sauce, finely chopped,
- 2 tbsp. of the adobo sauce
- Juice from 1/2 medium lime
- ¼ tsp. of kosher salt

Cooking Instructions:

1   Place all the ingredients in a medium bowl and stir to combine.

2   Cover and refrigerate at least 30 minutes before serving to allow the flavors to meld.

Scrambled Chickpea and Spinach Pitas

Preparation time: 5 minutes

Cooking time: 15 minutes

Gross time: 20 minutes

Serves: 8 to 12 people

Recipe Ingredients:

- 6 (15 oz.) cans of garbanzo beans, drained and rinsed
- ¼ cup of coconut oil
- 1 medium onion, diced
- 2 medium red bell peppers, cored, seeded, and diced
- 2 ½ tsp. of ground cumin
- 2 tsp. of ground turmeric
- 1 tsp. of garlic powder (no salt)
- 1 tsp. of kosher salt
- 6 cups of baby spinach, coarsely chopped
- 6 regular-sized pita breads, halved to form half moons

Cooking Instructions:

1   Add half of the chickpeas to a food processor fitted with the blade attachment and pulse until broken down but not puréed, set aside.

2   Heat the coconut oil in a 12-inch (or larger), high-sided skillet over medium heat until shimmering.

3   Add the onions, stir to coat with the oil, and cook until soft, for about 4 to 5 minutes.

4   Stir in the bell peppers, cumin, turmeric, garlic powder, and salt, and cook until the peppers are tender, for about 4 minutes.

5   Add the mashed and whole chickpeas, stir to combine, and cook until they begin to soften, for about 5 minutes.

6   Stir in the spinach, cooking just until wilted, for about 3 minutes. Remove the pan from the heat.

7   To serve immediately, divide the chickpea mixture between the pitas, filling each half with ¾ to 1 cup of the mixture.

Bean Soup

Preparation time: 10 minutes

Cooking time: 8 hours

Gross time: 8 hours 10 minutes

Serves: 6 to 8 people

Recipe Ingredients:

For the soup:

- 8 cups (2 quarts) of water
- 1 bag (about 1 lb.) of dried bean blend (not bean soup blend)
- 1 ½ to 2 lb. of smoked ham hocks, ham bone, or turkey leg or wings
- 1 medium yellow onion, small dice
- 1 cup of peeled and diced carrots
- 1 cup of diced celery
- ½ tsp. of dried thyme
- 1 bay leaf
- ¼ tsp. of freshly ground black pepper

To finish:

- Apple cider vinegar
- Salt
- Coarsely chopped fresh parsley leaves

Cooking Instructions:

1. Place all the soup ingredients in a 6-quart or larger slow cooker, making sure everything is submerged in water.

2. Cover and cook on the Low setting until the beans are tender, for about 8 to 10 hours.

3. Using tongs, transfer the ham or turkey onto a cutting board and let cool slightly.

4. Meanwhile, stir the soup, taste, and season with salt and vinegar (1/2 teaspoon of vinegar at a time) as needed.

5. Remove the meat from the bones, shred, and stir back into the soup (discard the bones and any skin). Serve topped with parsley.

Kidney Bean and Coconut Curry

Preparation time: 10 minutes

Cooking time: 1 hour 30 minutes

Overall time: 1 hours 40 minutes

Serves: 2 to 4 people

Recipe Ingredients:

- 2 cups of dried kidney beans, soaked in water overnight
- 2 tbsp. of vegetable oil
- 2 medium red onions, chopped
- 2 medium tomatoes, chopped
- 2 cups of coconut milk
- 1 tsp. of ground cardamom
- 2 cloves of garlic, crushed
- 1 tbsp. of yellow curry powder
- 1 medium jalapeño, seeded and finely chopped
- Salt
- 2 tbsp. of coarsely chopped fresh cilantro
- Cooked basmati or jasmine rice, for serving

Cooking Instructions:

1. Drain and rinse the soaked kidney beans. Fill a large saucepan with enough water to cover the kidney beans and bring to a boil.

2. Add the beans and simmer over low heat until tender, about 1 hour. Drain and set aside.

3. Heat the oil in the same saucepan over medium heat until shimmering. Add the onion and cook, stirring occasionally, until softened, for about 3 to 4 minutes.

4. Add the tomatoes and cook for about 4 to 5 minutes. Add the reserved kidney beans, coconut milk, cardamom, garlic, curry powder, and jalapeño.

5. Season with salt, stir to combine, and simmer over low heat for 20 minutes. Garnish with the cilantro and serve with rice.

Tofu Poke Bowl

Preparation time: 5 minutes

Cooking time: 15 minutes

Overall time: 20 minutes

Serves: 1 to 3 people

Recipe Ingredients:

Tofu Poke:

- ¼ to 1/3 cup of tamari, coconut aminos or soy sauce
- 1 tbsp. of rice vinegar or lime juice
- ½ tbsp. of sambal oelek
- 1 tsp. of sesame oil
- 2 cloves of garlic, smashed and finely chopped or finely grated
- 1-inch piece ginger, peeled and finely chopped or grated
- 1/3 sweet onion, such as Maui onion, julienned
- 14 ounces of block organic tofu (firm or extra firm), cut into 1/2 inch cubes

Bowl Filling:

- ½ cucumber, sliced
- 4 radishes, sliced
- ¼ red cabbage, shredded
- 1 avocado, diced or sliced
- 1 tbsp. of sesame seeds, toasted or black
- 2 scallions, white and green parts, sliced thinly on the bias
- Lime wedges
- 1/3 cup of roughly chopped cilantro
- Dynamite Sauce, optional
- 1 ½ cups of cooked rice (brown, black or cilantro lime rice) or quinoa

Cooking Instructions:

1   Drain the tofu and place it on its side, cut in half down the long side.

2   Place on a clean dish cloth or between paper towels and gently press to soak up some of the moisture.

3   Dice the tofu into ½ inch cubes. In a medium bowl or shallow dish, combine the soy sauce, sambal, sesame oil, garlic, ginger and sweet onions.

4   Toss in the tofu and let rest in for 10 minutes. Prep the remaining ingredients and assemble your bowls.

Chicken Brown Rice

Preparation time: 10 minutes

Cooking time: 20 minutes

Overall time: 30 minutes

Serves: 2 to 4 people

Recipe Ingredients:

- 4 chicken breasts
- 1 tablespoon of unsalted butter
- 2 ½ teaspoon of olive oil
- 2 medium broccoli (cut into small florets)
- 1 cup of zucchini (sliced)
- 1 cup of baby tomatoes (halved)
- 3 lemons (juice extracted)
- 1 tablespoon of pepper powder
- 1 tablespoon of Italian seasoning
- 10 cloves of garlic (minced)
- 2 cups of brown rice (cooked)
- ½ cup of cilantro
- 4 lemons (or lime) wedges
- Salt to taste

Cooking Instructions:

1   Cook brown rice until nice and fluffy. Once cooked keep aside to cool. Add juice of 1 lemon, salt to taste and ½ cup chopped cilantro into rice.

2   Give it a gentle mix. Marinate chicken breasts with lemon juice, salt to taste, pepper powder, Italian seasoning.

3   Mix well and let it sit in fridge until use. In a pan heat a teaspoon oil. Stir fry broccoli florets seasoned with little salt for about 2 minutes or more.

4   Remove from pan on to a plate. Stir fry zucchini slices in the same pan for a minute or so. Remove zucchini on to a plate.

5   Throw in the baby tomatoes and let it blister in the pan, takes about a minute depending on the heat of the pan.

6   Add the butter and remaining olive oil. Arrange marinated chicken breasts in the pan. Add minced garlic on sides of the pan.

7   Cook chicken on both sides until seared well. Remove from pan once cooked, let it cool. Slice. Portion chicken, rice, vegetables between 4 storage containers.

8   Top it with some more cilantro leaves. Serve immediately, or cover tightly with lids and refrigerate for up to 4 days.

Acknowledgement

In preparing the "Complete Meal Prep Cookbook", I sincerely wish to acknowledge my indebtedness to my husband for his support and the wholehearted cooperation and vast experience of my two colleagues - Mrs. Emily Cook, and Mrs. Alexander Bedria.

Debra Wetzel

www.ingramcontent.com/pod-product-compliance
Ingram Content Group UK Ltd.
Pitfield, Milton Keynes, MK11 3LW, UK
UKHW011322060125
3971UKWH00050B/848